THE JAZZ

MUSICIAN

THE JAZZ

EDITED BY

MARK ROWLAND AND

TONY SCHERMAN

ST. MARTIN'S PRESS

NEW YORK

MUSICIAN

Photograph of Wayne Shorter by David Redfern/Retna Ltd.; Ornette Cole-
man: Ebet Roberts; Lester Bowie: Darryl Pitt/Retna Ltd.; Charlie Haden:
Charles Stewart; Wynton Marsalis and Herbie Hancock: Deborah Fein-
gold; Chet Baker: Luciano Viti/Retna Ltd.; Miles Davis: Ebet Roberts; John
Coltrane: Herb Snitzer; Jaco Pastorius: Ebet Roberts; Sonny Rollins: Andy
Freeberg/Retna Ltd.; Tony Williams: Rick Malkin; Dizzy Gillespie:
Charles Stewart.

Design by Judith A. Stagnitto

Library of Congress Cataloging-in-Publication Data

The jazz musician / edited by Mark Rowland and Tony Scherman.
    p. cm.
    Interviews and profiles originally published in *Musician* magazine.
    ISBN 0-312-09499-X (hc).—ISBN 0-312-09500-7 (pb)
    1. Jazz musicians. I. Rowland, Mark. II. Scherman, Tony.
    III. *Musician* (Gloucester, Mass.)
ML385.J2   1993
781.65′092′2—dc20   93-10638
                                                CIP
                                                  MN

First Edition: August 1994
10 9 8 7 6 5 4 3 2 1

CONTENTS

FOREWORD

"Writing about music is like dancing about architecture." I forget who said that first, but it was probably a musician, serving all would-be Boswells a generous slice of humble pie. Anyway, it hardly matters, because anyone who writes about music regularly has moments—or years—when he or she feels the same way. Music may be the universal language, as another saying goes, but it gets pretty darn cantankerous when we try to translate its appeal into the one we use for everyday communication. More than a few stylists, straining for descriptions to take flight with the same grace and profundity as a John Coltrane solo or a Miles Davis blues, have instead found themselves sinking into a familiar quicksand of useless adjectives and spent metaphor.

What's a writer to do?

Well, write about the musicians, for one thing. For while the wonders of music, or the wondrous things music does for us, are often too mercurial to be properly bottled in prose, the vessels of such glory are real people—a breed of characters who are a lot like you and me and at the same time mysteriously apart, special. (Heck, we named our magazine after them.) Figuring out what makes them tick is a task that has challenged the best and the brightest writers working in the field of popular music today. Over the years we've been proud to publish some of the results.

But sculpting a profile of a great jazz musician is, in my opinion, a particularly slippery task. For here we are dealing with the crown jewels of this nation's culture, music that is at once distinctly rooted in African-American traditions and at the same time so commonly compelling that its influence can be heard around the globe. It is a supremely spiritual music, and so its greatest practitioners are the chosen ones, chosen in a way that's at once beautiful and terrifying to contemplate.

They are men and women betrothed to an art that requires the intelligence and discipline of European classical tradition, and also the emotional spontaneity and soul-baring of improvisation. Their genius recognized in far-flung locales, they often toil in relative obscurity at home. Indeed, the more rigorously they pursue their ideals, and refuse to be seduced by the material rewards of the pop music mainstream, the more likely they *will* toil in obscurity, and become objects of controversy within the small but passionately opinionated circle of other musicians, critics and fans who comprise "the jazz community." Their chances for riches and fame, compared to those stars of contemporary pop or rock or rap or country music, are a joke. Their reward is the magic they kindle for others on the bandstand, and the brand of zen self-knowledge such experience provides. Oh yeah, and the flicker of "immortality" that usually occurs right after they shuffle off this mortal coil, finally bequeathing their record company a suitable "hook" to reissue all their out-of-print records.

Writing about someone like that is no small thing.

Of course it is no substitute for the music either, as any fan would testify. But like a stolen smile, or an artist's brush-stroked portrait, a writer's perception occasionally opens the window to a deeper understanding and appreciation of a subject. And for anyone who's been moved by the music of giants like Miles and Trane, Chet Baker, Dizzy

Gillespie, and the rest of the royal cast who inhabit this book, there's at least the purely human pleasure of spending time with familiar strangers, whose ability to transcribe our deepest emotions has made them part of the family.

As for the writers, I suspect their reward is getting to hang out with great artists who make as little money as they do. Having worked as a pal and editor with most of them over the years, I can at least attest to one thing they share, which is a degree of reverence for this music and for the people who make it that can probably qualify as a religion. That is, they care enough about their subjects to make them come alive on the page.

As you know, we are living in the age of the instant celebrity, and of the transfer of the popular medium from the printed word to the video screen. Neither trend is very good news for fans of what was once a magazine staple, the in-depth biographical article. To call some of these profiles definitive is, unfortunately, less than complete praise, for this kind of writing rarely gets published anymore. All of which makes *Musician* doubly proud to present it here. Like the musicians whose lives are circumscribed in this volume, it may not represent the fashion of the moment. But there's still something to be said, I think, for quality that endures.

MARK ROWLAND
JUNE 1993

24 SHORTER SOLOS

BY DAVID BRESKIN

■

Chanting, chanting, chant-

ing like singing wafts into the den. With it, the fra-

grance of fresh-cut flowers, incense, and fish frying in

the kitchen. For the next half-hour Wayne Shorter's

spiralling song of devotion snakes through the house,

washing over the Japanese watercolors, the Joni

Mitchell photographs, the book of Folon prints, the

gold records of Bitches Brew *and* Heavy Weather,

the Lyricon and Prophet, the grand piano and stack

of freshly filled staffs on its bench. . . .

Listening, I drift back into Shorter's ripsaw tenor in Art Blakey's band, his hard-bop horn launched with Jack Kennedy's rockets. Thrust, pressure, liquid fuel, an arcing ascent into the bright blues sky of Coltrane sun and Rollins moon. The right stuff for a jazz messenger, higher, burning hotter in the thin air of rising masters. And with Miles, into orbit—each revolution, each pass across America more elliptical than the last. Blackness, blackness, the cool friction of orbits above Tony Williams, heat shield of the sixties. Farther still, after tearing dreams of supernova and steaming jungles of the heart, Major Wayne demands a weather report. Space shuttling 'tween arrow soprano and teardrop tenor, Shorter in asymmetrical equilibrium, weightless, letting less do more, moving beyond Milky Way. Boxer with Blakey, Bauhaus architect with Miles, Buddhist of boogie-woogie waltz, army sharpshooter at Fort Dix, mysterious traveller: telescopes of tradition search him out without success: off-center, untrackable, brilliant but invisible, soundings for a cosmic cartographer: no more notes. Shorter and shorter solos, Shorter lost in space, Shorter rechristened: Mr. Gone.

The earthbound critics, peering as usual through the wrong end of their binoculars, howl in dismay and *disappointment*. Jack DeJohnette's '78 composition, "Where or Wayne," becomes the more critically convenient (though nonexistent) "Where Is Wayne?"; Joe Zawinul and Jaco Pastorius are deemed contemptible plotters, driving Wayne, *our* Wayne, from the yearly Weather Report discs; one respected critic even panfries Shorter, in *Down Beat*, for falling into "routine" by "comparing" his solos on two recordings of "Black Market" (*Havana Jam* and *8:30*), which do indeed sound similar—largely because they're the same take. What have you done for me lately? What have you done for me lately? Manure dumped on the drought-stricken lawn of Shorter's art.

Lately, truth be told, Wayne Shorter has been writing his rear off. He wrote a piece called "Twin Dragons" for Miles's long-expected new album (Miles to Wayne, long-distance: "I asked you for a tune and you gave me a goddamn symphony!"). He's writing an album for Stan Getz, which Getz will probably record with a Swedish or Israeli orchestra. He's written new music for his next record, due out in late summer, which will feature Brazilian contralto Elis Regina and may involve *Double Fantasy* producer Jack Douglas. At the same time he's been compiling a "story-book" of new material for Weather Report: his own "Whole Earth Catalog of music," as he puts it. And if anyone thought his instrumental capabilities had deserted him, his playing on *Night Passage*—the most recent Weather Report—should close that case. Shorter's tenor wit and audacity boost *Night Passage* to the same altitude as '74's *Mysterious Traveller* and '72's *I Sing the Body Electric.*

Shorter stops chanting. Outside, clichés of spring chirp and flutter, promising rain, green grass, new tunes, saxophone rebirth, a good conversation. Over the next two days I'll meet his mother, wife, and daughter at home, and his good friend, Kareem Abdul-Jabbar, at the Roxy for a Gil-Scott Heron set. (Gil was married in this same den; Kareem was the best man.) I'll hear the man from the Brazilian consulate at the front door, and hear Miles trumpeting over the telephone. I'll hear of Wayne's love for his neighbor and portraitist, the husband of his first wife, Billy Dee Williams, and of his visit to "Strav's pad" (read: Stravinsky's house) back in the Miles quintet days. I'll see a report on the space shuttle on his large-screen Sony television and see him hard at work at the piano. And I'll remember mostly his sly laugh and his odd humor, and these solos, which speak for themselves.

I used to see Lester Young when I was very, very young. I had no saxophone. I was about fifteen, and he'd come with Jazz at the Philharmonic to a theater 'round the corner from where I lived in Newark. I'd get together with some guys and we'd go up the back fire escape and sneak into the theater. There'd be Billy Eckstine opening up with Stan Getz, and Charlie Parker with strings, and Lester would have the finale.

I noticed that Lester Young was different from *ev-ry-bo-dy*. He was always late. The show was long on and here comes Lester ... walking into the theater lobby. And he was the only one who used to carry the saxophone in a bag too. The rest of the guys had big, heavy, hard cases. His bag was shaped like a saxophone and he had this black overcoat and his porkpie hat and as he was walking in everybody—all the promoters—would run down into the lobby, yelling, I remember this, "There he is ... there's the *Prez*!!"

As soon as Prez came onstage, it was "Yeeeaaaahhhh!" I didn't know what these guys were "yeahing" about because I'm fifteen, listening to the musicians who played *flashy* things. I didn't see at fifteen the depth of where he was coming from. As time went on I found out Prez started a lot of things, and a lot of sayings that people started to live by or watch out for. He would say, "Watch out for the tiddy-boom"—once, a drummer was playing too loud and Prez took the mike and said, "No bombs, bay-be, no bombs ... just tiddy-boom, tiddy-boom." You know, "Ting te ding, ting te ding. No bombs, baby, no napalm."

I met him years later at the Town Tavern in Canada when I was just out of the army. He said, "Let's go downstairs to the cellar and get some real cognac out of those kegs." We went downstairs and he made a toast, grabbed some cognac outta one of those faucets—he got a double or triple, I got a double or triple—and we drank it. Then he went back to work.

As time went on I met his niece, Martha Young. She told me a lot about him. She would say, "You know one thing? You remind me of Uncle Bubba." His name was Uncle Bubba, she told me; "Yeah, he's a Virgo just like you."

Lester's style was all-encompassing. Charlie Parker listened to—not even listened to, but *observed* Lester a lot. He hardly moved his fingers on a horn. Or when he walked into a room, same thing, you'd hardly see him come into the room. He walked with his feet close to the ground. He didn't scrape them. And he never made a false move; if somebody came into a room to surprise you, or upset a household, he'd be the last one to turn around. Not deliberately, not trying to be cool. He'd turn around and say, "Heyyyy, what's happenin'" or "Don't you belong in the hospital?"

Anything that was very disruptive, Lester kept it inside himself. That's why no one knew he was sick, really sick. Curtis Fuller was one of the last people with him when he died. Curtis *never* knew. But he knew Lester was going to die if he kept drinking; drinking, drinking, drinking. Curtis had to call the ambulance.

THE FATHER'S ARMCHAIR

I remember when I was about fourteen I used to listen to "The Make Believe Ballroom" on the radio. It came on at seven-thirty every evening. My father used to come home from work, sit down in his armchair, turn the radio on, and it was Martin Block's "Make Believe Ballroom," the announcer would sing . . . "because it's 'Make Believe Ballroom' time!!!" He'd play Fletcher Henderson, Cecile Noble, something by Tommy Dorsey, Bing Crosby, Virginia

O'Brian—she was an actress and comedienne—Margaret Whiting, Barbara Whiting, Doris Day coming up through the big band thing, Billie Holiday, Louis Armstrong. Then one night he said, "Ladies and gentlemen, we'd like to try something a little different tonight. In life everything changes, so we're gonna play a new kind of music, from now on we're gonna play three or four of these records each night, see what you think about it. They call this music . . . bop." Boom, straight to the music, I think first Monk, then Charlie Parker, then Bud Powell.

I was playing the clarinet. I liked the sound of the clarinet. I listened to classical music a lot; I loved when the orchestra would cut out and you'd hear this lone clarinet, like in Rimsky-Korsakov, sounding like it was going over the sand dunes. I said, "I want one of them *horns*, I don't care, give me a *horn!*" My grandmother, my mother, they got together and got me a clarinet. Before that they got me a little tonette. My mother came home one day and she had bought a tonette.

CORN ON THE COB

Newark was a hell of a place to learn something about how to survive a lot of things, whether you were well off or very, very down in the dregs of poordom. Poordom. There are only a few people from Newark now who are somewhere in the world, imparting their knowledge of survival intelligently.

The people from New York always said that the people from Newark who *got out of there* were slick. And they'd say: slick, hip, and *crazy*. And it's a funny kind of craziness. We'd all go from Newark to New York and to Birdland, and when we started doing that, we found out that Newark itself didn't give us anything. We were learning how to get out of there. We knew there was a fight going on with the mentality: We used to go around telling people, "You are *cor-ny*, you're putting down the so-called bebop. You're putting it down and you don't know what you're doing."

We were stone beboppers. We were talking about progressive *everything*. There was a group of us that had found each other. And some of the people in the group melted back into the very things we were trying to destroy. The way to have a party, or the way to go out on dates. We'd say, "Why you go out on a date on *Friday* night?" We were being *fresh*. My brother and I put signs on our saxophone cases. He had a saxophone, too. We changed our names, he called himself "Doc Strange," and I put on mine, "Mr. Weird." We thought it was necessary to be weird, 'cause no one else was weird enough.

A FEW GOOD MEN

I was drafted right after I graduated high school. Just before I had to report to Fort Dix, I went into New York to a jam session at the Cafe Bohemia. I stood with my saxophone way at the end of the bar. Max Roach stood next to me. Charlie Parker had just died. Cannonball had just come to town and he walked in. Jimmy Smith came in, brought his organ in there in a big ole truck. Art Blakey was there playing drums, Kenny Clarke was there, Oscar Pettiford was on the bandstand . . . it was like a turnover. Sonny Rollins came through there that night. And Max Roach said, "You're the kid from Newark, right? Bring your horn on up." And I did. And I figured this was the last time I'm gonna play in my life, because I'm going into the army, and I had my draft notice in my back pocket, and man, all this stuff was going on. So I said, "Well, at least I was on the same bandstand with all these guys."

THE SUBWAY, 1950S

When I was in music class at NYU, the teachers would give me assignments and say, "If you want to experiment, do it on your own time and do it outside of class. When you're in class you have to do it the way it is supposed to be done." But a few of us would do an assignment and sneak in what we wanted anyway. And they would say— they didn't exactly know what was wrong because we'd sneak it in so well—"This is incorrect." Sincerely, they thought it was incorrect. But they didn't know what was going on in my mind. You know what I mean?

Except one. One teacher. She said, "This may be incorrect, but it's all right. I know you're sneaking around on the subway doing all this stuff." We used to ride the subway and experiment; "Hey, why don't we move this C sharp over here, and let's do some perfect fourths *anyway*" because they said we couldn't do that. And we'd try to hide 'em. But that one teacher would catch 'em. Every time.

HEY JOE

Fifty-second street, Birdland, right on that corner. The first time I met Joe Zawinul he'd been in New York less than a month. He'd heard about me, wanted me to be in Maynard Ferguson's band with him. I don't remember talking that much, but it seemed that Joe and I talked without talking. I drank so much that night that I didn't remember he couldn't speak English very well. He was just happy to meet someone over here who shared some similar thoughts.

THE DEVIL LOOK

I played in Maynard's band with Joe and Slide Hampton for about four weeks. Then we were up in Canada at a big festival and Art Blakey was there. Hank Mobley wasn't—

he was in the band but he wasn't there, so Lee Morgan came right up to the bandstand when we were done and said, "Hey, man, you want to play with us?" I'd met Lee one summer, I was just out of the army, and Lee and John Coltrane came to Newark to play on their night off. It was a Monday-night special, "John Coltrane from the Miles Davis Band and Lee Morgan from the Jazz Messengers." Someone said to me, "Better take your horn, man." I took my horn. John was just starting to explore that sheets-of-sound stuff and Lee said, "Hey you, the guy from Newark, come on up." He always had that little devil look, and he was *looking* at me. So later when we saw each other, he never forgot. In Canada, he said, "Hey, come on, man, what you doing in a big band, man, come on." So I joined Art Blakey's Jazz Messengers and Art said, in that gravel voice, "The guys seem to dig ya. I know about you, too." I knew about two tunes.

DESERT BOOTS OVER TOKYO

The only thing I had on my mind was getting that horn together, getting a distinctive sound, not being a general tenor sax-sounding guy, general tenor sax-looking guy. And Art knew that. He would say, "Let's go down and get some custom-made suits. We don't wear uniforms, we wear *suits*!" He wanted something special, and that band was a terror because we walked out onstage with some blazers and all—we broke new ground as far as how you appeared. We wore desert boots and in Japan they put them in the showcase windows; they said, "This is what Jazz Messenger wear." And we knew that we were something 'cause Miles didn't want to be on the same bill as us.

Miles would call up in the middle of our rehearsals. Blakey would answer the phone, he'd say, "Miles want to talk to you." He'd say, "See there, Miles trying to steal my tenor player." He first called in '61, but I stayed with Art until '64. Miles got George Coleman 'cause I told Miles I wasn't gonna desert the band that I'm in, that nobody likes a traitor. And Miles would go, "I can dig it, I can dig that." Because he dug some integrity.

49 INTO 64

People said, "Hey, that's a helluva change going from Blakey to Miles," but it really wasn't so hard. I knew what to do about changing styles: I was like an actor playing a different role. I knew what kind of teamwork, what kind of method was needed for the Messengers—hard bop, *bombastic*, man, hit it! Now Miles was different, but I'd been rehearsing or practicing at home and in hotel rooms and in the army, practicing the horn with pianos and violins and stuff like that, so that I already knew what Miles and all his different bands were doing. I used to play with his records and blend, start to blend right in. It's like with an orchestra player: He might go from playing *The Rite of Spring* to *Daphnis and Chloë*, or from Gustav Mahler to Erik Satie. I was prepared, I was ready to go. And early on, during a break, Miles came to me and said, "Do you feel like you can play anything you want to play, anytime, anywhere, just play *anything* you want to play?" I said, "Yeah, just about." He said, "Yeah, I know what you mean."

Though no one could accuse me of rehearsing for five years with Art Blakey to go with Miles, Miles's whole thing had been a part of my life since I was very young. I'll show you something I drew when I was fifteen years old—it has some of the feeling, some of that sensibility, sensitivity, Miles had, and the way Herbie played the piano as opposed to the way Bobby Timmons and all those cats played. This is a comic strip I drew. This was 1949.

The "comic strip" is a rather thick book of blue pen

drawings entitled Other Worlds. *There are launching pads and space suits and rockets and monsters and warfare and whirlpools, and one dapper-looking future-man pointing out of the frame and saying to another, "Note the texture of her hair." The drawings are precise, intricate, clean, and crumbling from the press of time. Note the texture of her hair: Milesesque indeed.*

WHIM, THE MUTHA OF INVENTION

By the late sixties, we knew we were on the verge of something. Herbie said, "I don't know what to play no more." So Miles says, "Don't play nothin'. Only play when you feel like it." So we'd be playing a piece of music, and Herbie's sitting there with his hands in his lap . . . then all of a sudden he'd play one sound, and Miles said, "That one sound you made was a bitch." So everybody saw *something* happening . . . and we began playing songs without chords. Tony Williams then melted into the rock-jazz-swing thing, Lifetime, and I saw at that time maybe something more elusive, which came on *Super Nova*. Elusive, but not so elusive as to be uprooted out of the earth, the earthiness of life. At the time all this was going on, I could see the changes happening—but I couldn't really know the depth, the gravity of them.

First of all, there was that recording of *Nefertiti*. Joe Zawinul said when he heard that, he knew he wanted to hook up together. I remember being in the studio doing *Nefertiti*, we kept repeating the theme and not soloing, we kept repeating, and Miles said, "Do you feel like soloing?" I went, "No, man, I don't feel like it," so Miles just said, "*Oh, shit,* let's keep repeating it." And Tony Williams just kept bashing. It was, "Ohhhhhh shit!" and I remember thinking, "Uh-oh, nobody else is doing this." In between *Nefertiti* and *In a Silent Way* there was a complete 180-

degree turn. And then *Bitches Brew* came along. That's when Miles sent for John McLaughlin. I got a picture of him playing with us on the wall, see? I said, "Here comes Prince Valiant." He looked like Prince Valiant then.

Now, Now, Child

We spent a whole evening at Joe's apartment in New York trying to come up with a name for our cooperative group. I said, "Let's have a name that people are confronted with every day; how about 'The Six O'Clock News'? They have politics, and sports, and the weather forecast." We decided to stay out of the political arena, the racial arena, and the fortune-telling thing. I heard "Weather Report" and everybody, simultaneously, said YEAH! You report *exactly* what's happening *now*—as opposed to forecasting what's gonna happen. It leaves no room for ulterior motives or anything. It's very, very difficult to report exactly what I think *right now*.

We knew we'd be together for a long time, but not ever doing something so stale that we'd have to break up. We said we'd be together as long as it was fresh; fresh and exciting, and when it's happening, it's only because we're doing individual things. And we'd say, let's get together later on and make it an event—another Cecil B. DeMille movie, bam!! This way we can give so much more when we perform than if we played all year long together, dropping our grain of rice into people's lives with the attitude "If you see us all the time, it must be worth something." It doesn't work like that. And if you're playing all year round, you can't write anything new—even if you write something new in your hotel room, it'll be the same music. You may think it's new, but it's probably an extension of something you're already doing.

Weather Report has honed some other planes, other

sides of planes and surfaces. We've tried to give some kind of alternatives for feeling about something or someone. When you play our music in a house, some people for the first time may think of music as interior decoration. Maybe we've done musically what certain designers have done, those that go further than design, those that go to the soul: exterior decoration of the soul, interior decoration of the body. That's pretty good. . . . That came out like a child.

THE DROUGHT

Material that's written, that's the life of the band, it's just as important as the expression of the material. So Joe has been asking me to write more because that would give more dimensions to the band, so that we can keep our personalities more colorful. Joe would like me to do, say, 85 percent of the writing—but I was struggling. I was struggling, trying to write—starting about four and a half years ago—trying to break through, wondering who else is like this, in the world, struggling and struggling? For the first time it was very painful trying to write. I've heard about painters who would stop in the middle of the canvas and say, "That's all. . . . I have nothing more to paint." That's how I felt. I was worried I'd gone dry, permanently. I'd wonder. And sometimes I'd talk to Miles and he'd say, "Yeah, man, I know what you mean: If there ain't no more, there ain't no more." [laughs] Miles was glad to have some company.

Everyone talked and wrote about the onslaught of my partners, Jaco and Joe, but that's wrong. It was something I was going through myself. Other aspects of my life were developing. I was going through a metamorphosis, like the pain of being born. Parts of myself, which had been stunted for a long time, started to grow, and they met resistance. If value is being created in your life, you meet a lot of resistance. A lot of resistance came in the form of "Hey, you're not taking care of your music, you're not the one-hundred-percent musician you're supposed to be." But I let everything go, I didn't try to do *forced* music, which would have been catastrophic, to commit that kind of suicide. When you talk about someone's *life*, that's a helluva thing: to talk about somebody's life in terms of just how much music somebody's writing, or how many plays, or how many films.... I would say the heaviest struggle I've had in my life has been the last four and a half years.

A CHILD IS BORN

Iska. That's Iska in the kitchen. She was given a vaccination when she was a baby. And they called it vaccine pertussive something—for the arteries in the brain. And she had an allergy to the shot, so that now she has brain damage. Over the years it's caused me a lot of pain, and that's another reason I started practicing this Buddhism. I've tried to break through some things, no matter what it might cost: It might cost a lot of publicity or negative comments, or people wishing out loud, "I wish Wayne would get up off his butt and take charge. Man, he used to be one of the top composers." And I'd say, "I'd like to hear him play, too." But it takes a human revolution when you start to do something because your daughter's got brain damage and you can't do anything, you feel like you can't do anything about it. But when you try to do something really valuable, you always meet with resistance, and it will erupt in your *entire* life—which cuts across everything you do—in your music, *everything*. We try to change the negative thing to a positive thing, to make the most value out of it. We call it changing poison to medicine. Not *avoiding* the poison—you drink it—but you change it to medicine. You face it.

I mean, you can't ignore the notion of karma. Why are we together, Iska and I? Why are we linked together? Iska was normal for three months, until she got that shot; I said *never mind* the shot, her life came in this condition to change ours, to open our eyes. It's very funny, but it's like ... Iska kicking my butt, and at the same time, she's contributing a helluva message to us, every moment we look at her. She's fortifying us, she's helping us become indestructibly happy—even in the face of droughts and external catastrophes. We don't live in fear of earthquakes or what people might say. Iska's got a message, especially now, in the past year, she's made me try to take care of *everything* 100 percent—put 100 percent into everything. It grew, it was a growing message, so that naturally now it comes. Now I don't have to be really torn up about going on the road and her being here. But there will always be someone with Iska twenty-four hours a day, for the rest of her life. It's already set.

SHORTER TAKES

"Chaos," "Genesis," "Go," "Yes or No," . . . Juju, The All Seeing Eye, Playground, Footprints, Tears, Milky Way, Wind, Storm, Calm, Joy, Marie Antoinette, Tom Thumb, Sincerely Diana, Lester Left Town, Elegant People, Schizo-phrenia, Paraphernalia, Miyako, Twelve More Bars to Go, House of Jade, Mahjong, Free for All, Adam's Apple, The Odyssey of Iska, Freezing Fire, Super Nova, Limbo, Nefer-titi, Armageddon, Sanctuary, Chief Crazy Horse, This Is for Albert, Orbits, Dolores, The Moors, Shere Khan the Tiger, El Gaucho, Night Dreamer, Sweet Pea, Eurydice, Beauty and the Beast, Blackthorn, Rose, Hammer Head, Africaine, Port of Entry, Children of the Night, Charcoal Blues, Black Nile, Capricorn, Harlequin, Face of the Deep, Pinocchio, Water Babies, Palladium, Umbrellas, Deluge Montezuma,

The Elders, Lost Surucucu, Manolette, Three Clowns, Moto Grosso Feio, Antiqua, Ana Maria, Iska, Non-Stop Home . . .

RIGHT TO LIFE

A tune? It comes like a sound, a note—it comes like a person. And first it's like a person without eyes and a nose, and if you discard it, it's an abortion. But if you stay with it, stick with it, all of a sudden the note becomes a real person and the person starts pointing his fingers to the next—and there's another note. The one you're writing tells you what the next person is gonna be like, and then the whole thing has its own life. And it's a natural feeling.

Right now my improvising is intricately related to my writing. It's very related now because I'm investigating—not new harmonic structures or anything like that—but the way different harmonies go together. Once in a while I take the chance to pick up my horn, and I feel something different happening with expressing the improvisation *throughout*, and over and underneath and around, the kind of harmony that I'm writing now. I'm incorporating scoring, you know.

THE BODY ELECTRIC

One thing I've found out about the synthesizer is that it doesn't quite yet have the tonal weight of the acoustic instruments. There is a kind of transparency after a while with the synthesizer. But we will get to the point when it won't matter, because the synthesizer will no longer be sounding like or competing with acoustic instruments. It should compete with itself and become a whole—another kind of weight, another kind of body and texture. The only one, except for maybe Tomita, who gets the full weight out of the synthesizer right now is Joe Zawinul.

Well, I have something about that whole electric vs.

acoustic controversy. I think that electricity has water in it. Electric neutrons or something like that, protons or neutrons, whatever they call them, whatever goes on: There's water *inside* them. Ha! So where there is water, there is acoustic! I mean, you know, it's like a little room that's moving around, a little room that's on fire.

NON-STOP HOME

I've been listening mostly to movie soundtracks recently. I like some of the sounds John Williams gets in *Close Encounters*. Remember the ending, when those little things are coming, making way for the big ship? There were some great musical nuances, because my mother—she's sixty-eight—she's in here watching it one day, and she said, "Dear Lawd"—she talks like that, you know—"He's gettin' down with those sounds, honey!" And I said, "Yeah!" 'Cause the music started to swing with the visual.

Outer space? You know what attracts me? The security of it. Space tells me there ain't nothing to worry about. Even though you might worry about things, you still got that as a home. That's home too, you know. This home is only home because that's home, ultimately. It's exciting to have that much room for unlimited adventure. So when you go out that far, you ain't going nowhere but home.

THE LITTLE BIG BAND

A lot of the strength of Weather Report's playing—our playing all *together*, not just individual soloing—is because of our tone quality. Jaco's got a certain unique sort of tone, and Joe started getting really outstanding synthesizer tone qualities, and I have a style, a tone quality, which in the mid-seventies was mostly coming from the soprano sax—and the tone quality seemed like it wanted to pull us ahead to be on display, for itself.

A lot of other groups, they would have the soloing on top, mainly because of the thinness of the tone quality. One person would have to take a turn, you know, individual solos one after the other, in order for each instrument to have that kind of *presence*. What I'm saying is that our tone quality *allows* us to play more freely.

The "less is more" thing, that was quite right, because I was investigating some things. With a particular tone quality, you might not want to continue playing long, drawn-out phrases. At some point the best part of the tone quality that you have *rings out*, but doesn't stay long, so my phrases were short for that search, that quest. Today the audience may experience something different, because I'm right on top of a tone quality that's more conducive to "*more* is more." I'll probably be playing longer phrases, and that "less is more" formula will not apply from this point on.

F-14

Improvising to me is like ... say you're captain of a big commercial three-hundred-passenger jetliner; improvising to me is like getting in a fighter plane. Same guy, no passengers. Solo! So-*low!* And going for total speed and destination. The trouble with being a big airliner, see, is you've got to regulate your speed and destination. But when you improvise—ain't no room for passengers on that trip.

SWEET SCIENCE SWING

I'll tell you a funny thing. Joe saw me working out one time and he said he thought that if I had gotten into the ring I'd have become a champion boxer. He felt the same way about himself, and about Miles, of course. I haven't seen them move like boxers, but what they do rhythmically, and what Sonny Rollins does, would make them good in the ring. And it's the same thing in reverse with a boxer, like Archie Moore. We used to correspond a lot, a whole lot, and I think Archie Moore would have been a good bass player or something like that. Some boxers I know, they *know* music.

THE SPACESHIP

What makes me happier than anything? Music? No. When I see a lot of other people happy, like when I see the group now, and all our families. We've all come through a lot of personal things and we're holding together over the years. Families, domestic things—this makes me happy—everybody still pulling together like in a big spaceship of people and we all still have the individual things that we are, and we all overcome obstacles. That's the kind of happiness that keeps refueling itself. It can't be destroyed. Maybe it's someone overcoming something in the hospital, maybe it's someone overcoming something to write a composition, you take that and then you go out and play somewhere and you play with greater *gusto*.

ANA MARIE SHORTER SPEAKS

Ever since I was a girl, I've had a big passion for Miles. He calls from New York nearly every day. We talk to him. Maybe he and Wayne might rehearse something together over the phone. A few weeks ago, I called Miles at the studio. He played me a ballad, like I haven't heard him play for seven years. Well, I *screamed* and *cried* so loud. It was beautiful. And Miles said, "What a fool!" But then he went around telling everybody, telling the whole world, "Man, Ana Maria *cried*, Ana Maria cried." I did. I cried that day—it was one of the happiest days of my life. I was so happy to hear his life again, because that's what you hear in music: the essence of a life.

When I first met Wayne, he was real weird. I met him

through his music; it was love at first listen. That told me a lot about the man, his music. Then I met him in person, at the Bohemian Caverns in Washington; he was playing with Miles. I was eighteen. I was after him, and when a woman is after a man, it's only a matter of time until she gets what she desires. I'm from Lisbon, Portugal, and I came from way far away to this country to meet Wayne Shorter, what else. Destiny. And I asked him to marry me. *I* asked, of course. He's not as weird anymore; he's focused his life a little more, he's more in control.

He was drinking hard when he was with Miles. He'd sit up at the bar, ordering doubles and triples. Now, mind you, he was a very quiet man. He kept everything inside himself. He was a very sad man—coming out of his first marriage—but he was writing beautiful music. Even after drinking, he'd pick up his horn and play the shit out of it. But later on, it began to affect him, and our marriage, and then I started to drink. And you can't have two. Wayne always told me being on the road is the loneliest thing; I guess drinking filled up that hole.

Wayne had a long drought. It was hard. He was entitled to it; he took the time to take care of other things in his life, away from music and Weather Report and whatever, and now he'll take those things with him. When I'm upstairs and I hear him downstairs and hear the music *pouring* out of him, I think, "MMMMMMM ... fantastic!" He gets up early, he's given up drinking. He hardly ever smokes a cigarette. He eats and writes music. You wait ... he's gonna bombard the world again.

WAYNE AGAIN

I think the high point of my career is coming. Moments higher than before are coming, they're on the way already. I have two good horns now, I have the tools; and I have the valuable breakthroughs, crashes, changes, and turnovers in my life that were brought about by me, sifted out by me, and are all my responsibility from here on. I'm going up on hill number five. I'm going for it now, going for it the right way.

TOOLS

I've got a new horn, a new tenor. It's got a sound that's outtasight. It's gold-plated. My silver one sounds more tentative, the gold one is beautifully balanced. It sounds like a swordsman's horn. It's like Jim Bowie's knife, you know, made from a meteor, made from a star. This horn has the styles I want to travel through. This horn has flight in its sound. That's what I like about Coltrane's sound — he has flight in his sound. I think with this sound I can make a lot more notes sound like just a few. I'm gonna use both onstage.

I'm also getting myself a completely new instrument that an inventor, a young Russian guy, has been working on for ten years. There's no name for it yet; for the convenience, they call it the Synth-a-phone. But I call it the magic wand. It's gonna have touch-digital stuff, and on the back there's twenty-six keys and buttons and rollers, like a bassoon. It has two or three things, like a Wave Bar, which are first-time-in-history features. The inventor is the same guy who made that big Tonto synthesizer and helped with the Oberheims and invented the insides — the guts — of the Prophet. It costs as much as a grand piano and I should get it any week now. The first one is for me.

—July 1981

23

ORNETTE COLEMAN:

GOING BEYOND OUTSIDE

BY QUINCY TROUPE

Ornette Coleman is one of the most influential musicians to emerge in the post-bebop period. The possibilities he opened up for improvised music in the late fifties and early sixties, when he scrapped the conventions of Western harmony and pitch for a conception that was both a leap into the future and a recovery of the blues past, show no signs of being exhausted, and the implications of his more recent work, involving symphonic composition, free-funk, and the "harmolodic" system, are now being worked on by a new generation of musicians, many of whom are alumni of his bands.

Born in Fort Worth, Texas, on March 9, 1930, Coleman has been an enigma for many years inside and outside the music world. Loved and respected by many, he has nonetheless been maligned for his ideas and innovations, particularly in his first decade of public life. Even more than John Coltrane, Cecil Taylor, and Eric Dolphy, Coleman served as a magnet for the charges of charlatanism that raged in the free-jazz wars of the Sixties, but his formidable talents as both instrumentalist and composer have made his place in the history of instrumental music secure. Only Louis Armstrong, Charlie Parker, Miles Davis, and Coltrane have had a more dramatic effect on the practice of jazz.

His conversation resembles his music in its disregard for linguistic convention and for the liberating effect it can have. A certain amount of editing has been done on the transcript, but the greatest number of conceptual knots have been left untied. Coleman understands how things harden and ultimately die of the sense people make of them (see his discussion of method below). His inventions have always tended to subvert the usual dead verities. His first classic band, a quartet with Don Cherry on trumpet, Charlie Haden on bass, and either Billy Higgins or Ed Blackwell on drums, simultaneously developed and obliterated the parameters of bop. When this quartet broke up, Coleman was fugitively audible for the remainder of the Sixties with a trio, occasional R&B band, or string quartet. He had begun to simplify his playing style (see his distinction between "improvisers," whose strength is in their lines, and "players," who communicate through their sound). In the early Seventies, he was even less available to the public, appearing occasionally with a quartet and even more occasionally with a symphony orchestra, as in his long piece, *The Skies of America*. In the middle of the decade, he began working with an electric R&B band, Coleman-style, called Prime Time, with which he recorded the seminal *Dancing in Your Head* and the (hopefully) soon-to-be-released *Fashion Faces*, and with which he has begun to concertize this year. Coleman has never had trouble making great music, but liaison with the material and economic world has run from shaky to nonexistent. Even in his absence, his influence has been extraordinary and undiminished. Currently managed by Sid Bernstein (of Beatles-at-Shea-Stadium fame), he is with us again.

It's said that the desert camel can feed on the thornbush when water keeps the thorns green and alive, but that when that plant dies the dry and darkened thorns lacerate the camel's tongue, and he dies. Through a subtlety of disposition that combines an almost childlike naïveté with a percipience more acute and truthful than that of the conventional intellect, Coleman has succeeded in keeping his music alive, nourishing, and unpredictable. This interview took place in the offices of Sid Bernstein in New York City, on July 22, 1981.

MUSICIAN: *Let me begin by asking you: Do you think that your absorption of bebop was and is one of the difficulties people have in understanding your music?*

COLEMAN: I didn't make my first record until I was twenty-eight or twenty-nine but I'd been playing bebop since the late Forties. It got dated for me, at least the style of it. I had figured out where I wanted to go, myself, musically. The reason I was having problems was I was trying to do *that*—go someplace else musically—more than trying to prove to someone how that involved bebop language. So, many musicians didn't approve of me playing like that, and at the same time I wasn't having any jobs to prove that I was someone that people wanted to hear. Whenever I went to a jam session I would try to play the bebop line, but when I got ready to solo, I would play exactly the way I'm playing now, today, which is exactly how I played when I first picked up the horn. Musicians thought I had bebop all screwed up the way I was playing the lines, but I had figured out that most bebop songs were lines interpreting standard songs by using standard changes, but with more advanced lines, you know? I understood that it—bebop playing—was a *method*, and when I understood that method and had really absorbed it, I found that I could keep the method in my mind and still play independent of it. The method for playing bebop had become stronger than the *creativity* of bebop. With Charlie Parker, Bud Powell, and Thelonious Monk, bebop was their expression. It wasn't a method to them. It was their expression, it was what they did. And everyone else, including myself, was playing *their* method, and I had learned their method, the method of bebop, very well; I could play and sound like Charlie Parker note for note. I realized that regardless of how advanced I was going to play bebop, I was *still* only going to play it from the method. So I banned the idea that I was going to be a very successful bebop player. I accepted the fact that, okay, now that I've observed and absorbed this, now where to go? And then I remembered when I first got my horn I was playing ideas without having to relate to anything. I thought that maybe if I did this I would, perhaps, find something.

MUSICIAN: *Did you find something?*

COLEMAN: I started with the saxophone, especially the alto. I found out when I played an idea the way I was approaching it—which was outside of the way people were telling me to approach it—I didn't have to transpose the notes to sound right with the piano. The piano key—like a C concert piano—would put the alto in A; therefore, A-minor and C are the same sound when you're interchanging your method of using them. That's the first signal I got about how I was approaching the saxophone. Instead of thinking of the alto as a transposing instrument, I started thinking of it as a concert instrument. For instance, if you're in the key of C in the piano, that makes your alto A natural, because there are six above to get the same pitch, right? But yet you have the same notes without worrying about that pitch. That's what I was doing: I was playing everything in what I thought was concert. I later found out I was only playing in the concert key of *alto*, not the concert key of piano. I realized then that melody not only is something a person thinks of to manipulate on the instrument, but it almost by design is a hard sound according to the instrument you're playing it on. *Melody*, right? A person playing an African thumb piano and a person playing an electric piano are going to have two different ideas about melody, only because of the instrument they're playing.

MUSICIAN: *Because of the technique involved?*

COLEMAN: Yeah. And the instrument. I started analyzing the difference between the alto sax being in its own concert key as opposed to transposing. Then I came up with the term "harmolodic," which I call the harmony, the melody, the time, and the rhythm all having equal positions. I got involved in writing music. You see, I finally realized that the *method* set up the musical patterns in bebop, so that if you had a particular song that you liked, a standard, for instance, like "Laura," you'd say A-major 7 to to E-minor 7 to B minor. And if you played those voices without playing the melody, you would resolve the voices according to how you heard your horn sound through those voices. I said, well, if that's the way the standard song is played, then what would happen *if the instrument became that itself?* In other words, if the sound of the instrument was what you were making, the voices sound like more than the melody you were trying to play. I started playing ideas as if I wasn't playing the saxophone—it was just an instrument, but not an instrument that you had to transpose on, you know? I found that I was having much more trouble playing with piano players and other musicians because I would be in one unison and they would be in another. I started understanding the complex voicings of how and why musicians choose certain instruments to play, and it has a lot to do with how they've been related to concert instruments. I'd been playing sometimes with piano players where the piano would be so out of tune that I'd have to play out of tune in order to be in tune with their out-of-tuneness. It only brought me back to that same problem of playing nontransposed sound, you know? So I started writing music that people could play with me so they could understand how that sound was.

MUSICIAN: *How did musicians and people respond to you and your ideas then?*

COLEMAN: I found a lot of negativeness in the community I was playing in, black and white. They were all saying that this wasn't the way music and the saxophone were supposed to be played. And they weren't seeing it as really putting me down; they really believed from where they were at that I was wrong. I didn't try to show them that they were right or wrong. The only thing I tried to do was see if I could find a way to bring the sound of what I was playing to where they could get something out of it, and I knew, given the chance, it would work.

MUSICIAN: *Do you think it might have had something to do with the fact that you wanted to be Ornette Coleman rather than Charlie Parker during the bebop era?*

COLEMAN: I met Charlie Parker; I liked him and I enjoyed his songs. But I wanted to have the experience of him hearing what I had done, because by the time we met, in 1951 or '52, I was really into what I did later on my own records. But I couldn't have any attitude about what I was doing—especially with Charlie Parker—because no one had ever given me any attention to think of it as something that was valuable to them. I had always made compromises just to play bebop. But it kept working against me, because regardless of how long bebop has been around, it still didn't reach a success level commercially the way Louis Armstrong was a success. And bebop today, despite critical acclaim, has still never gotten any real big musical play in the way that fusion music has.

MUSICIAN: *How did you and Charlie Parker interact?*

COLEMAN: I was around twenty-one or twenty-two when I met him. I met him in Los Angeles at a club he was playing on Eighth Street and Normandy. He was only playing standards; he wasn't playing any of the music he had written. But when I heard him playing standards, it blew my mind because I didn't expect it and because I understood so well the method he was using to play his ideas. What I remember about him, though, was the fact that he knew very well he was the musician of the era; it was in his attitude toward himself and whatever he played; he knew exactly what he was doing: He was in total control. I got the feeling from him that he didn't have any problems with his talent, you know? I didn't know then what his personal life was—I later found out that it was pretty bad—but then he was at ease. I got the feeling from him then that I later got from myself; that he hadn't found the outlet, business-wise, that would have brought him to a wider public. I felt that he was still being limited. He and I had the same problem: The money people don't know you, hardly any of them are aware of this music because it isn't commercially viable to them.

MUSICIAN: *What has made you commercially "unviable"?*

COLEMAN: I found out that I was constantly being limited by the term "jazz." This was around 1976. By this time I was writing symphonies, music for string quartets, woodwinds, etc., but the critics were always telling me how "great" a "jazzman" I was. But I was into other things. This limiting bothered me. I thought about how every time I played in public I was always writing a new musical program. I thought this was my duty to an audience—to write new material every time I played in public—because I though they wanted to hear something they'd never heard before. Then finally, at the Public Theater in New York this summer, I went out and played something I already recorded and got a big response from it. I said, "Oh, this must be the way." I'd never had the experience of someone liking my old music in public because I had never played it. I didn't realize I could play my *own* music and get the response I got at the Public this summer. Most of that music was off of *Dancing in Your Head*, which I recorded in 1976. It became clear to me that I could play music I wrote twenty years ago and music I wrote yesterday and have people that knew the old stuff and people who wanted to hear the new stuff enjoying both things.

MUSICIAN: *You and Coltrane and Miles Davis have had a tremendous impact on contemporary instrumental music. But in terms of the "fusion" movement, I think you and Miles have created two different but similar musical languages that are both fusionistic and futuristic at the same time.*

COLEMAN: Let's start with Trane, because I always had a good experience with him. He used to come and visit me a lot and I, him. About three or four months before he passed he sent me a check and a note and said that he had finally found it, and thanks very much. I never got to see him again. Let me say it this way. The improviser, the person that's called the improviser, has been the maverick of musical expression in the modern civilization that we call the Western world. The improviser is known as the jazzman, and he's been the one who says, "Just give me the horn and put me in front of the people and I will take this horn and do something better than what you can prepare or compose in a structured way." But for me, the improviser has become less and less interesting, because of the *method* and style of what improvising is; it is bogged down, for the most part, in some personal, social background. Take Albert Ayler. Now, I knew Albert very well, and Albert was a musician that really was very gifted, one who did not relate to any form but his own. What happened to the kind of music—free-form—that Albert was associated with is that it became connected with the racial phenomenon that took place in the sixties. Critics started saying that this was black expression, a kind of social, black expression of, perhaps, rage. Right? But when Trane started playing this music it brought the critics back to thinking of it just as music. They didn't do this with Albert Ayler. With Trane it was a musical expression, which it was. It was just more demanding to listen to, more so than bebop. The music of the sixties really stretched out; the improvised form had never gotten so individual as it was in the sixties, and the kind of music I was playing—even the writing sounded like it was being improvised. I started trying to let the themes finally become improvised. I started trying to let the themes finally become even freer than improvising. I was trying to get more free than the structure of improvising had previously allowed. *But then that too was becoming a method.*

MUSICIAN: *Are you saying that people run the danger of becoming the method in any kind of music, or expression, even if it's supposed to be new?*

COLEMAN: That's what I'm saying. I have always wanted to move forward. For instance, in 1962 I hired a rhythm and blues band, a string quartet, and my own trio, and performed an original work at Town Hall. I started playing with them not thinking of fusion or anything, but because

I wanted to have more color to improvise from, to get away from thinking about improvising. The more voices I had to inspire me, the freer I felt I could be from improvising. I went from there to writing for string quartets and symphonies because if I could create enough sounds in unison, then the listener could see the difference and growth between where I started from and where I was then.

MUSICIAN: *And where was that, where were you going then?*

COLEMAN: I realized that the multiple expression could be translated into sound where you could hear and sense more than one thing at once. I assumed that I could write a musical idea that would interject more than one particular direction, where musicians and the audience could have more intake, and that this would be more enjoyable to do. I went and bought me a trumpet and a violin and I started playing those instruments. I started putting those things into the music I was writing. Back to your earlier questions about fusion: By this time Trane had passed, and Miles came out with this rock band that sounded just natural to me. This was in the early Seventies, and by this time the music was moving toward fusion.

MUSICIAN: *What were some of the other changes that were taking place in the music during this time?*

COLEMAN: Well, in most music, pop, etc., time is dominated by the drums. In the music I was starting to play, *every* instrument, every person had the right to dominate.

MUSICIAN: *Every instrument?*

COLEMAN: When I heard fusion it only made me realize that Miles and the people playing fusion had taken the roots of the drums and used it as a form of improvising with whatever melodies they were playing. I had always been doing that, but not in a systematic way. It was then that I realized that it had always been the improviser that had stood out as the jazzman. But understand; the improviser and the player are two different people. I've always wanted to be a player, myself.

MUSICIAN: *What's the difference between an "improviser" and a "player"?*

COLEMAN: Okay. For me, Johnny Hodges was a great player, rather than an improviser. Charlie Parker was a great player, you know? But I think Johnny Griffin was and is a great improviser. I think Jackie McLean is like that—a great improviser.

MUSICIAN: *What would you say about Coltrane?*

COLEMAN: I think that Coltrane was about half and half. Great improviser, great player.

MUSICIAN: *Where would you put yourself?*

COLEMAN: Like I said, I think I'm more of a player.

MUSICIAN: *What would you say about Miles Davis?*

COLEMAN: I think he's more of a player than an improviser, though he can be a great improviser, too.

MUSICIAN: *That's interesting. What about Julius Hemphill and Arthur Blythe?*

COLEMAN: I think they're really improvisers. I think that that's a group of musicians that whether they are backed by instinct, or by sweat, it comes out that way—more like improvisers, rather than like players. I think the trumpet player Olu Daru is a great improviser. But you understand that improvising, to me, is almost self-annihilating. I mean, you know your limitations. As a player you don't really know your limitations that way, because the construction of playing is like architecture—you are always building, you know? Where improvising is like the person who's always putting furniture in, who's always putting this and that in, and sometimes you only get a jumble of stuff that doesn't relate to anything.

MUSICIAN: *Do you think "improvisers" can become "players"?*

COLEMAN: Yes. I think I was an improviser once.

37

MUSICIAN: Dancing in Your Head *has real funk in it, heavy funk, almost honky-tonk and gutbucket in places.*

COLEMAN: You see, all the things I grew up with back in Fort Worth, Texas, affect the things that I play. There was honky-tonk, blues, and funk there, so it comes out naturally in the things I play. That's why I am a "player," because when I picked up my horn, I didn't think about improvising; I thought about *playing*, I've always thought about playing. I have always tried my best to stay clear of having a particular style. For some reason, improvising doesn't have a style, but a style has improvising.

MUSICIAN: *Are you saying you don't want, ever, to have an identifiable style?*

COLEMAN: Yeah. I wouldn't like to have a style.

MUSICIAN: *But there are musicians—Coltrane, Blythe, yourself—that as soon as I hear them, I know who they are.*

COLEMAN: I know, but that's pitch. When I hear your voice, I know that's you. I think that what you're talking about is the character of a person's breath marks. It's in their pitch, in the pitch sound. I don't think that makes the sound better, though. Look at Paul Quinichette and Lester Young. The only way you can tell Quinichette and Lester apart is that when you hear Lester you get an emotional experience from that sound, and from Quinichette, you get a remembrance; he's just making you remember where you heard that particular emotion from. But it *sounds* just like Lester. I can play like Charlie Parker all the way down to his sound because I know the things to avoid and the things to touch to create that sound. And I am sure someone that wished to repeat the things I'm playing could do it if they really wanted to. The only thing different in the way I'm playing is that I don't use any structure to play that way.

MUSICIAN: *Do you think it's very difficult for some other alto saxophonist to duplicate your sound?*

COLEMAN: When someone plays ideas in logic, in the same logic as I would, it's much easier to do. But when you play the same idea without that logic, it's harder. And that is what I'm trying to do; to play logical ideas without using logical terms.

MUSICIAN: *How would you explain the "harmolodic" theory?*

COLEMAN: What instrument do you like? What is your favorite instrument?

MUSICIAN: *I like saxophone, trumpet, bass, guitar; I like most of the musical instruments.*

COLEMAN: Okay. Let's say we use a string instrument, like the guitar. On the guitar you've got six strings. When you want to make a sound you pluck the strings and they vibrate, right? But *there's an order that's already there, on the instrument*; the order that is designed and made is already there. So if you play something that makes you feel good, you think it's you, but all you're doing is playing something that's already there. In "harmolodic" theory, or music, I suggest to everyone: Don't think that just because there is something you want to play, and the instrument that you want to play it on, you have to put your mind to working out something only to make mistakes until you find out what you're really doing. The thing is to acknowledge the fact that the instrument is going to respond the way you approach it, right? So, basically, the only way you can approach any instrument is to find the relationship between the sound you want to hear from it and the place you have to put your mouth and fingers to bring about that sound. Now, the only thing that keeps you from doing that is the *method* that's already there on the instrument, how that instrument was built to play in the first place. So in "harmolodics" what happens is that the particular method, the sounds that you want to play, or the ideas, say on a guitar, might be trumpet ideas in your mind. So what I tell the person is that whatever instrument you want to play, just think of the music that you want to play more than how you want the instrument to sound. Once you find the place to put your fingers and carry the sound to the next sound, you will find yourself playing in a sequence. And most all Western music is written in sequences. When you start learning music, you find out these sequences are called chords, they are called keys, and they are called changes; they're called lots of things. The thing to realize in "harmolodics" is that you want to manipulate it—the idea on the instrument—and then you find out the limitations of the instrument.

MUSICIAN: *So the musician takes the initiative on the instrument, bends it, so to speak, to his will, to what he wants to do with it?*

COLEMAN: Right. If you brought me an instrument I'd never seen, never played, I wouldn't try to figure out what the traditional role for playing that instrument has been, but I would try to figure out what I could do with it just from knowing it's already built to play whatever it is designed to play.

MUSICIAN: *You were saying earlier that the drums have dominated the time in music at one point, and that you wanted everyone in your band to have the chance to dominate. Could you talk about that a little more?*

COLEMAN: The word "dominate" is not the right word. In classical music, in a symphony orchestra, you sometimes have thirty to forty different instruments. Now, imagine if those thirty or forty instruments were playing their own line, you'd hear many different ideas, right? But those thirty to forty instruments have been designed to only play, basically, four different voices, which we call in the Western world the bass, treble, tenor, and alto voice. What I mean by "domination" is that the rhythm concept is the only free movement in sound that doesn't have to have a strict pitch to be heard. In Western music, what's called the tempered scale, there is a strict pitch. If we're in the key of C, you'd have to produce that C and I would, too. Because of that strict pitch, musicians have been limited rhythmically. Whereas in the drums, Eddie Blackwell, Billy Rich, always played the rhythm as if it was as valuable as the note. A lot of drummers don't do this. They play notes over rhythm.

MUSICIAN: *What about young drummers?*

COLEMAN: The person, for me, that has taken the drums to a more advanced place is Denardo.

COLEMAN: *Your son Denardo?*

COLEMAN: Yeah. Now Denardo, for some reason, can play a set of drums the way African people play talking drums. On a talking drum, you can reproduce the actual melody, with the sound, and independent of the rhythm at the same time. Denardo uses the concept of what talking drums must have done before drums had to establish a regular sense of time.

MUSICIAN: *I remember when I first met you in Los Angeles back in 1967, you were getting a lot of bad press for using Denardo, because he was so young.*

COLEMAN: Yeah, I know. When I met you I was playing at Shelly's Manne Hole in Hollywood, and I remember Shelly Manne saying Denardo should go and become a "garbageman," or something like that. At that time, Denardo was not only playing freer than any drummer I had played with outside of Billy Higgins and Eddie Blackwell, but he was also inspirational to play with. The first thing I recognized when I heard him play was the way he saw the time, the way he saw keeping the time. He sounded to me like he had been listening to a lot of drummers, and although he had a teacher teaching him about reading and everything, it seemed to me that this hadn't affected the way he already wanted to play; it seemed to me that he already had his own concept of how he wanted to play, even way back then. He really enjoyed playing. I never tried to tell him what not to do, or what to do; the only thing I have ever talked to him about was how good he could get doing what he believed he could do best. He has perfected how to play the drums as if he was singing.

MUSICIAN: *Could you talk a little about your present band?*

COLEMAN: The band that I have now has two guitars, two drummers, and two basses. You see, I couldn't afford to have an orchestra, which is what I would prefer to have. The guitar is the most popular social instrument, especially to white people; it's what the tenor saxophone is for most black Americans. Anyway, the guitar takes up a lot of the string section. Having two of them usually means you use one for the rhythm and one for the melody. What I have done in my band is that the structure and the playing both interweave. For instance, if I give a melody to one of the bass players, I'll say I want to play the harmony equivalent, and I'll give the guitar that number. Everyone is playing a lead that's equivalent to the same results, so we don't reach a climax by someone being at a certain place at a certain time. That's the difference between "harmolodic" music and arranged music; the musicians don't have to be at a certain place with some rule reaching some climax. It can happen instantly and according to the way the mood and feeling of whatever we're playing dictates.

MUSICIAN: *Does Denardo play saxophone lines on the drums, and do you play drum lines on your saxophone, violin, and trumpet?*

COLEMAN: That's what I'm saying. I think he plays the vocal concept and the rhythm concept. That's what he does. And I do, too.

MUSICIAN: *So everyone is playing all kinds of different parts and voices at the same time?*

COLEMAN: Right. Everyone's also playing what they think would be best if they had their own band.

MUSICIAN: *How do you approach rehearsals, and how is new music brought in and introduced to the band?*

COLEMAN: What happens is that all of these guys have their own music, right? And, they would probably like to have their own band if they had the same outlet that I have. At rehearsals, I will write out a musical idea. I'll play it on the saxophone and then I'll have them play on their instruments the equivalent of what I played. Then I'll write it out. But the main thing that happens is the motive of the idea. Ideas are very interesting, but it's the motive behind the idea that's very stimulating. So if you get hung up in playing an idea, it might be outdated and not stimulating at all. For me what makes a musical motive is when everyone gets excited about how it affects them. If I brought in a new musical idea, it has no validity other than for it to be manipulated on the instruments. But when someone else shares in it, then it becomes really musical. And that is one of the great things about having a band: playing the music, exploring new frontiers of musical consciousness.

MUSICIAN: *What kind of music are you composing today and how long is it?*

COLEMAN: I am writing a piece of music, a long piece, for what I call the oldest musical language, and that's what it's called: *The Oldest Language*. The music will be for about 125 musicians, and for as many nontempered musicians as I can get into it. More than half of it is written. I think it would be at least two hours, maybe three, when it's performed. But I haven't thought about where I'm going to play it, or how I'm going to make the time to play it. If I get it done, I will play it somewhere.

MUSICIAN: *What instruments are you writing for in this music?*

COLEMAN: The talking drums. The sitar. The kind of

instruments African people play, instruments that Arabs play. Basically, string, wind, brass, and probably some other instruments made out of some form of metal.

MUSICIAN: *I know you're going to have Denardo's drums in this, right?*

COLEMAN: Oh yeah, right. Denardo's drums will be there, too. But the thing that I'm more interested in is having the experience of hearing the musicians express how these sounds are going to affect how they play as an individual. That's the result I'm looking for, that's my motive behind doing this. And what I hope to bring about is, shall we say, some form of medicine in the music.

MUSICIAN: *Medicine? Could you explain?*

COLEMAN: What I would hope for is that some kind of healing medicine would be incorporated in these sounds, come from these ancient instruments. I would like to try and bring about some kind of medical sounds that could actually cure depression, cure whatever it could. I think that some certain people outside of doctors do this now, already, but it's done in such a camouflaged way, you know?

MUSICIAN: *So you think music can cure?*

COLEMAN: Oh, yes.

MUSICIAN: *Why did Shannon Jackson call you a "magician"?*

COLEMAN: Well, maybe he was using that word for describing how I think. I don't think of myself as a musician, or composer, but as a human being that has the same problems everyone else has, in that I have to figure out how to do my share in this human state we call living. I think that maybe Shannon was giving his philosophy about how he thinks I think about things I believe in. You see, I believe that immortality is distance, and that things take up more than just one-dimensional aspects of our living. I think that what we call the earth and human beings and the way we live and die is distance, you know?

MUSICIAN: *What do you think about the connection between your music, Blood Ulmer's, Shannon Jackson's, and "punk" music?*

COLEMAN: Well, I think that everybody can logic. But I don't think the label, necessarily, has to be transcribed. When someone says "punk rock," when you use any term that is nonmusical, you're really talking about a person, or a group of people. It's much easier to label a group of people than it is to label music. I saw the movie *The Decline of Western Civilization*. It's a "punk" movie. And what I got from it was that a lot of rich white kids that have grown up with human ideas are now using music to express violence. So if that is the particular signal they enjoy being stimulated by, then they will, or must eventually grow out of that, because violence usually leads to death.

MUSICIAN: *You have no animosities toward critics, no hostilities?*

COLEMAN: No, I don't have any. I always say I don't have any enemies, period.

MUSICIAN: *What about the experiences you had in Morocco and Nigeria?*

COLEMAN: When I went to Morocco, there was a festival they were having, a festival that had been handed down for the last six thousand years, and their music was as old or older than that. It was really beautiful. The same thing in Nigeria. I guess for some reason in a society like America, where the people haven't figured out a way to grow closer together, that basically it's the goodness of being a human being that transcends the structure of what someone doesn't want you to be or have. My outlook for being born in America and being an American person, I feel the same way as any person that's born in America, and being an

American person, I feel the same way as any person that's born—that where you are born has something very important to do with what you are born to live as, and that you don't have to imitate any race, or to force your race on another person, but to find a way to better the conditions of why you were born. These are some of the things my trip to Africa taught me, that I could be myself, because I didn't have nobody else to be.

—November 1981

LESTER BOWIE:

ROOTS, RESEARCH,

AND THE CARNIVAL CHEF

BY PHILIPPA
JORDAN &
RAFI ZABOR

■

I *might go back to Jamaica*

in another three or four years. I went down there after

I made this record Fast Last *in '76 or '77. That's what*

I used to do, make a record and then finance an expedi-

tion to somewhere. When I got to Jamaica I had a

new suit, clean trousers, I had the whole look and

everything, a room at the Sheraton, just enough money

to cover the airport and get a cab to the hotel. I got to

my room and bought all the newspapers and laid them

out to see what the scene was. People had given me a

couple of phone numbers, but my assets were just five dollars after I'd paid for the room for a few days. I went downstairs and there was a reggae band playing in the bar. I asked if I could sit in. After about three notes this guy said, "Hey, *brothah!*" Next day I had a crib up in the hills, in the mountains, stayed there about a year after that. I had all the musicians bring me out some trumpets and I had a workshop with all the local kids in the hills, this real small community. And they took care of me, if my food was running low, they would see to that: their parents would send up crates of mangoes and pies. I had a house and no money and I had these kids all the time. These cats were *bad*, chicks, too. They would play some fantastic stuff and they would learn so *quick*. I was a music man, and I would always be playing. If I wasn't playing all the time people would say, *"Hey, I thought you played trumpet!"* I'd get up in the morning about seven, go outside and practice and people would come out of their houses all over the hills, big valleys, you know, just dotted all along with houses and these people would come out and listen. If they didn't hear me by noon, someone'd come up and ask what had happened. The union made me an honorary member. I'd come into town about once a week, get high and sit in on all the bands. The only real gig I did was my own TV show. I had a TV show, it was an hour show, an hour special, a Jamaica TV special. It was *nice*.

If you play music, and I play trumpet, you're gonna attract some attention. I never worry about it because I can always deal somehow. Either that or you just die. I almost thought I was finished in Nigeria though. Nigeria almost got to me! I always wanted to go to Africa, and I got tired of just talking about it. I'd just done a European tour and when we were finished I said, "Well, I'll see you all later." I had some more money this time. I had one hundred dollars when I got there, then I had to spend fifty dollars a night, and ten dollars to eat. I didn't have enough money for the next night and I didn't know anybody in Nigeria. And Nigeria was really *out.* I thought, *This is it, man. You've done it! Finally you've bitten off more than you can chew! This is it!*" It was rainy season, fuckin' mud, but I made it. When in doubt I just get my horn out, see, and start hittin' it. I had a couple of phone numbers. And ended up with Fela. Once Fela heard me, that was it, 'cause that's the one thing I've always done, is just play.

NECESSARY INTERRUPTION

Although maybe after that story he needs no introduction. Revolved in the mind, Lester Bowie has the satisfying roundness of a fully realized fictional character hewing happily to his archetype, an actor who has found his human role and plays it to the hilt. Here is this guy in the doctor suit and Ming-the-Merciless two-pointed beard with his haunting tone, half-valve whinnies, and apparently endless articulations of the spirit of the blues: a perfect self-invention whose proper life assembles itself around him in hills and valleys dotted with houses and music, crates of mangoes, trumpets, pies. Seems like a real happy fella.

Most of us know him best as the trumpeter in the Art Ensemble of Chicago. Turn on the projector, please. There he is, onstage between Roscoe Mitchell and Joseph Jarman, lurching his way through a sudden sputtering funky interjection, swigging heavily from his bottle of Perrier, then swaying, head cocked back, to sounds unheard and heard. He is the strongest melodist in the band, and of the three horns the only one who has gigged in every idiom American music has to offer. Good Lord, this band plays some weird shit. Here's a second clip of him, this time wearing his immaculate, white, practically luminous chef's suit. Yes, he loves to crack the audience up. Look at the size of that hat. The soundtrack's bad, but you can hear him leading the band out of the gossamer and into the hot. Boy, they're great. You can turn it off now.

Let's take his style seriously for a moment. It is, I'd say, the most original and fully realized approach to the trumpet anyone has come up with in twenty years, and it is there, surprisingly full-blown, on his earliest recordings (*Sound* and *Old Quartet*, '66 and '67 respectively, both released under Roscoe Mitchell's name), when he was still in his mid-twenties. You can anatomize it if you like— the straight playing from Clifford, Kenny and Miles; tonal effects an inspired leap from the premises of Bubber Miley, Cootie Williams, Rex Stewart and Lee Morgan—but that only covers some of the ground and misses at least two main points: that Bowie's is a seamless approach to the resources of the instrument, and that he has invented things none of his ancestors remotely imagined. His work is a living lexicon of everything black musicians have done to make the trumpet their own in America, all the proud and sardonic defections from tonal orthodoxy—school's out—and European dominance that represent a triumph history has tried to butcher in the flesh but has been unable to kill in the spirit. Bowie employs all the resources of the exile—superior cunning for example, and a better sense of humor for another—to steal the world back from its dull, stolid, putative owners and make his stand and a free man's song. Sideways like Miles he skips the direct line from Armstrong to link up, probably, with mad Buddy Bolden, parades certainly, and the church, the prison, the back-porch, and the angry oven heat of the fields, so that while he is an extravagantly comic artist, his music carries its full cargo of history and humanity, a reconciliation of private anarchy and collective order. If the bones of his style were in place from its recorded beginnings, what has grown and deepened over the years is its body of implication and, as anyone who has listened to him closely these days can tell you, its beauty. Like Miles, he can go dowsing with one slender note and reliably find the heart.

With resources like these, naturally he works a lot. In addition to gigs with the Art Ensemble, which come a lot more frequently than they used to, he's led a fine series of quintets, worked with Jack DeJohnette in the New Directions band, organized the memorable Sho' Nuff Orchestra (fifty-eight pieces strong), recorded with Fela Anikulapo Kuti in Africa, jammed with the Bear at the Tin Palace and Roy Eldridge at Jimmy Ryan's, made records for Muse, Horo, Black Saint and ECM, organized lately a superb band called From the Root to the Source and most recently an all-trumpet extravaganza called the New York Hot Trumpet Repertory Company . . . he keeps busy. The Repertory Company, at the moment six trumpets strong and including among others Olu Dara and the remarkable newcomer Wynton Marsalis, is sort of a brass counterpart of the World Saxophone Quartet ("Yeah, and we'll whup their asses, too," said Bowie when I suggested an encounter). Root to the Source is the incarnation of a more enduring dream: to put all of Bowie's own music together in one band and send the wheel of it rolling through the world.

Bowie has a fierce and vociferous pride in his professionalism and the places it's taken him: the carnival tents, blues shacks, Jackie Wilson shows, weird Chicago stages—all the music on which he has never felt too pure to muddy his hands. He's managed to carry most of his experience into Root to the Source, and what is most important is that blues, gospel music and jazz are each presented authentically, not as superficial stylistic coups. Bowie's current quintet is augmented by the voices of Fontella and Martha Bass (his ex-wife and mother-in-law respectively) and the virtuoso gospelist David Peaston. Fontella Bass in particular, although nowadays she only sings in church outside of

Root, has never sung better. Neither has Bowie sounded more free; he has assembled the spokes of his musical world around him and is audibly at home in it, rolling.

Here, anyway, is this interview. Perhaps you already know what a great talker Bowie is, and there's a few thousand words of that. He also, I think, emerges as an enormously encouraging figure—I'd use the word inspiring, but it has inappropriately solemn connotations—for his totally positive attitude, his habit of working tricky heights without benefit of a net, and his outright refusal to take the world's ubiquitous No for an answer. Craziness helps, too; here he comes out of the night on his Harley in a lab jacket and Darth Vader helmet—Zorro! If it's an act, it's a good one. It probably takes a lot of work to be Bowie—the last time I saw him he sat tired backstage between Art Ensemble sets at the Bottom Line: "Sometimes it's like diggin' ditches, you know?"—and it probably would be naïve to imagine that he's sidestepped the daily drudgery of being human, but in the essentials he looks suspiciously like that rarity of rarities, a free man. If you were shopping around for a handy incarnation of the spirit of jazz these days, you could do a lot worse than mad Lester Bowie.

He's Coming Here from St. Louis

When I first started getting interviewed the guy asked me how long I'd been playing, and I had to think, I didn't really know. I had to go and ask my old man. He had been putting a mouthpiece or something in my face since I was about a baby. We decided that I really started when I was about five. I don't have any recollection of it, because I've just been playing all the time. My father, he had the uniform and the cap, did parades and stuff like that. Both of his brothers were musicians, his father was a musician, and that's going back a way to slavery, because my old man is seventy-six. So it goes on back, I don't know exactly how far, a whole line of musicians. I've got a picture upstairs of the band my father was in before he was even big enough. The original Bartonville Coronet Band. I've got about three uncles in that.

My father taught in school, but I was so bad he didn't want me around. Not where he had to work. He didn't let me go to the same school! I mostly played trumpet and got into mischief. We used to do all kinds of things, start up bulldozers and drive them around. By the time I was fifteen I was in the musician's union. I'd worked clubs by then. I was always in two or three bands, all the school bands, the All-City Band, the All-City Orchestra, the All-City Swing Band, All-City Marching Band, and the—I would go and play with the old cats, the veterans' bands. There were community centers that had bands and I did little church recitals, too.

But when I got into high school I started hearing about Bird. John Hicks was there and Phillip Wilson and Oliver Lake. We had some really hip musicians. Hicks was cool even then, he had a hip little trio, he had a suit and tie, he had that look. Phillip was cool, too. Phillip was like an organ trio–type dude. We had fun, but I didn't think it was the thing I was going to do for a living. I thought it would be crazy to try and attempt something like that. I didn't decide that I wanted to play trumpet until I was twenty or twenty-one. I looked up and I was twenty years old and never done nothing but play trumpet! I was in the service at the time. I had gone through a lot of experiences in the service. I was in the Strategic Air Command police, I was playing with the band, I was playing with a blues band every night in town as a civilian, I did a lot of shows and stuff on the base. Anyway, I ended up, I was in jail, in solitary confinement for something I had done, gettin' high on duty or something, 'cause I went through *every* kind of

part, from the police to prison. I had a ball in the service—
I would recommend the service to any young man—but it
ended up, "Now we're sitting in solitary." I had two weeks
of it and I said, "This ain't it! Whatever I've been doing in
the past, if it led to this, it's not happening!"

I'd been listening to Kenny Dorham. He sounded so hip
that I said, "I would really like to be like Kenny Dorham,
just a really hip trumpet player." Because he was really
hip, not just a regular trumpet player but a hip trumpet
player's trumpet player, and I thought I'd just as well do
that as opposed to what I was doing, which had me sitting
in solitary. I had been in every band they had since I was
that big, but it never had been like, "Seriously, what are
you going to do with yourself?" Now I was going to be a
professional. And when I stepped through that door . . . I've
been flying ever since! It's been unbelievable! You know it
beats working, beats the shit out of working!

STRONG BODIES TWELVE WAYS

I knew I didn't play well enough to be a professional. I
needed to have a couple of years of intensified practice, so
I went to school and did nothing but practice twelve or
fourteen hours a day, take pills and practice. I went to
Lincoln University, a regular black college and then I went
to North Texas State, a white college, the first school where
you could get a degree in jazz, so I figured they were slick
as scientists. I figured I'd see what they were talking about,
and when I was down there I got to hang out and play in
bands like James Clay, Fathead Newman, all the hip bands
in Dallas.

We were talking about influences. The way I play trumpet has been influenced greatly by Art Tatum, the way he
developed melody and played songs. Influenced a lot by
Coltrane and Sonny Rollins, by a lot of people that don't

play trumpet. Take the embouchure I use. It's flexible, whereas with standard trumpet playing you're supposed to get a set embouchure and stay with it throughout. Well, years ago, when I was going to school with Julius Hemphill, I noticed the flexibility of his embouchure—it almost looked like he was eating the saxophone mouthpiece sometimes, different things he would do to get different inflections. I started to adapt that to the trumpet, to put different emphasis on different parts of the horn, and this has been instrumental in the development of my style.

Just about everyone I've ever heard has influenced me. You have the trumpet players you were inspired by, that you read about—Louis Armstrong and Miles and Diz obviously—but there's another whole set of trumpet players no one's ever heard of who helped me. I think everyone has these two categories of influence, but it's never mentioned.

There was a guy in St. Louis when I was about fifteen, his name was Bobby Danzie and he was like jazz, very cool. Came up with Miles, you know, played his ass off and kind of took me under his wing. And I didn't really know anything at all, just a little fifteen-year-old kid. I used to go over to his place and he'd show me how to play songs, and some of the things he told me stuck with me all the way. Like he told me, "Lester, whatever you end up doing, *whatever* kind of music you play, you've got to be soulful." And then he'd show me. He'd show me how to get that soulful sound with a little bit more air in it, just adds a kind of really hip soulful sound with a lot of air. Cats like Miles, Gene Ammons and people, the guys with big, soulful sounds and the way they phrase, using the tongue for attack, he got me together with that, even before I knew what it *meant*.

There were guys like Johnny Coles who helped me a lot when I was in those R&B bands. He would show me how to play my part, interpret it, how to phrase. Marcus

Belgrave was another cat. Marcus was bad! He helped me a lot, still does, anytime I see him. Of course I've been influenced by Miles and all of that, but Miles didn't say how to roll your lip around a little bit or whatever. I just met Diz a couple of times. He still doesn't speak to me, just sneers when he sees me, you know. Freddie Hubbard, Kenny Dorham. Blue Mitchell was another cat.

I'll tell you something about Blue Mitchell. I was just starting off in the service and I said, "I'm not going to listen to *nobody*. I'm going to lock myself up here and practice and I'm going to get me some new licks that ain't nobody playing. *Nobody's* gonna influence me. I'm gonna develop my own thing!" I started playing. Then one of my buddies came and said, "Hey man, have you ever heard of this guy named Blue Mitchell? Well, listen to this!" On the record was everything I thought I had made up. I mean he had licks I couldn't believe, because I just knew I had made them up! And so then I learned that you can't close yourself off, and I've never been afraid to be influenced by someone. Some people are afraid to be, they think it will dominate their thing, but I think it's just the opposite.

Like Freddie Hubbard influenced me for awhile. I didn't know what I was going to play, because it seemed that Freddie was playing it all. I just took Freddie's solos and wrote 'em out in all the keys and I'd practice 'em for ten, twelve hours, to try to get some of the essence of what he does and then add it to myself. Freddie taught me how I'd have to be a good musician, and Miles taught me how original I'd have to be. I gained my manhood by checking out Miles. Because the way he plays, you'd almost have to be a trumpet player to know—most people, guys like Diz, play up and down, thirds, fifths, fourths—but Miles would be playing *sideways*. You can hear it, it's all kinds of sideways. That's why he's Miles, because he's got another thing.

58

Fats Navarro, Clifford Brown. I used to say that if Clifford Brown was still alive, I'd be working in the post office and Miles would be my supervisor!

THE CIRCUIT

Fast Montage: Let's see, when did I get that gig with Oliver Sain? Fontella and Oliver were part of Little Milton's band. . . . I'd play with Albert King, a lot of touring with Little Milton, twenty-five one-nighters a month. Ike Turner was in town, producing records for Fonnie, then she hooked up with Chess. "Rescue Me" and it caught on from there. I was her musical director for the next few years, I was making plenty of bread. Jackie Wilson, the Apollo Theatre, that theater circuit, the Regal and the Apollo, the Royal in Baltimore, the Howard in D.C., the Uptown in Philly. I think the Riviera in Detroit. Different blues sessions. I'm on a lot of those old sessions they made at Chess, I was never listed. I had money and a big house, I was in Chicago quite a while before I ran into the A.A.C.M.

WEIRD CATS/NICE GUYS

I always knew there was other stuff I wanted to do. When I was at the carnival, the cats thought I was crazy. I was like this young cat, up early in the morning and practicing. I worked for this carnival in a tent, and that was the hardest gig I ever had in my life, musically, physically, and I've had a lot of experience in tents. For a while the Art Ensemble lived in tents. We got to where we could live damn near anywhere. Comfortably. That really helped the Art Ensemble, all of us were army veterans, knew how to fix our meals on the road.

Well, what happened is, when I got to Chicago I was doing all this different stuff, and I was always saying, "What else is happening?" 'Cause these guys were playing their parts and that was about it. I fit in, but it was kind of boring to fit in. A baritone player named Delbert Hill took me to a rehearsal of the Richard Abrams Experimental Band. It was shocking, because I hadn't seen that many weird cats in one room before. There were twenty cats, all the cats, Roscoe, Joseph, I met them all at the same time. I'd always run into some, there's always those isolated cats, three or four cats, but I'd never seen that many of them in the same place . . . and *playing*. You can go that much farther if you've got just a few people that are like-minded and go out and play. The collective is a more interesting way to live. Especially when times and conditions are adverse, you can manage to survive in a collective. Respect is a very important point in that context. You've definitely go to have respect for other people. If you've got that, you can actually do something. You look at the Art Ensemble—*these guys play weird music.* We've been together longer than damn near anybody in the business.

We took various trips before Europe. Europe didn't just come up out of the clear blue. We had traveled extensively in the States and Canada and parts of Mexico before '69. On our own, barnstorming, hitchhiking, all over. I rode a bike, I rode from California to Chicago and back on that. Roscoe and Malachi followed me in the VW bus full of instruments behind this BSA. I used to really dig it when I had that. I could play, then speed off into the night. It was a nice fantasy, and I enjoy fantasy so much . . . the shit's gonna be bad next time! I'm gonna get a bike with every-thing on it, everything, and I'm going to have all the latest in leather, and a helmet like Darth Vader. There's a helmet now just like Darth Vader. It's bad!

When I met the Art Ensemble, the only person besides myself whose income depended entirely upon music was Malachi, who worked the Holiday Inn. The rest of the cats, they played, worked in factories and had other jobs. I was playing for a living and immediately my whole objective was to be able to make the same kind of living off the kind of music we played with Roscoe. We had gotten as far as it was going to go in Chicago. We decided to go to Europe. I want to emphasize that any group can't just pack up and go to a foreign country and survive. For nearly four years before that we had been traveling, we had recorded, we had quite a bit of experience as a group before we went.

I had a Bentley and a house full of fabulous furniture and everything that went with that whole scene in the sixties. I figured if I sold all of that, I'd have enough to take the whole group to Europe, so we made a deal. The cats borrowed the money they needed and eventually they all paid it back. Roscoe was ready, he was tired of working. We had to talk Favors into it, he didn't want to go—but it takes all kinds of thoughts to make a well-rounded group. If no one's reluctant, if everyone's ready to go, maybe no one's thought it out thoroughly. Anyway I had some material things I could put my hands on to get money, and the only way we could do what we did was that we had bread. When we went to Paris, we had a country home surrounded by cherry trees and plums and grapes and we had rehearsal space and rooms for all of us to live in. That was at St. Luc-le-Forêt, our first house. We were expelled from France after our first year. We were asked to leave by the police. Someone in Luxembourg was doing a radio show about us, not an interview of us, and it was like the Art Ensemble, the Black Revolution, the revolution and yes, by the way, they live in St. Luc-le-Forêt. And one of the big cats, who was the big commissioner or the Duke that runs that section, said, "What! Here? Get 'em out!" The next day the police, this Inspector Richard—trenchcoat, straight-ahead shit—went in and saw this cat in a uniform. It was weird, but it fit right in because we were leaving anyway.

We lived in a tent, but we lived hip. Hip sleeping bags,

we had all the right stuff. We had a whole caravan of trucks, we had formations we got into with them. We were even selling trucks for a while. We went all over Europe like that, from way down in the south of France up to Scandinavia. I don't want people to think we've ever lived bad. We carried our own environment, we were eating fried chicken and barbecue. People couldn't believe the food, they would come and eat with us and hang out. You may not have money all the time, but that doesn't always make, you know . . .

New and Old Gospel

We don't feel that we have to limit our sources of reference. That's a drag. The things I do I feel naturally. I don't put a big thing on playing jazz, or playing blues, I just play music. I like it all. I feel free to refer to anything that runs through my mind, without all those preconceptions. I don't think I should be put in a role that I couldn't like gospel music. In this band I've got now, the Root to the Source, how do these gospel singers sound with Philip Wilson on drums and all these different people? Well, it's killing!

There's Donald Smith, Hamiet Bluiett, and Fred Williams, and the gospel singers. Martha and Fontella Bass and David Peaston. You think of Great Black Music as a tree, and you get all of these roots—gospel, blues, jazz, rock—and they all merge into this single trunk, and then its branches and flowers would be reaching to the source of what's happening. It's another form, another feeling, when you experience all these emotions in the space of an hour, it's devastating almost, it's unbelievable, when you think back on what you've felt. I mean I've seen some people completely wiped out, in tears, that couldn't even speak English, so I *know* it works. We've been to Australia and Europe. We had four thousand people at our last concert in Sardinia. I mean four thousand people going crazy! We're dealing with Great Black Music, and we have to recognize that, it benefits everyone. We have to get above isolating parts of it and saying, "Well, this part of it's okay, but this part's not too cool." We're not that far away from the source. You have to realize it's taken several hundred years to get this far.

We realize we're dealing with visions, and we can deal with visions in sequence. You can structure the feelings, and it doesn't have to be a chronological thing, it doesn't have to be "Here comes the blues and here comes the gospel." It can start with the avant-garde and end with the blues. I mean, I know the audience, they aren't dumb!

If you're going to play the blues, you've got to know about playing the blues, you've got to have damn near lived that sort of thing. If you're gonna be in a bag, you've got to be *in* it. When I play, I try to play everything I've heard or felt. I didn't spend all that time in the carnival never to do that again, or all that time playing blues to push it to one side and say, okay, I'm avant-garde now. I didn't learn all these damn chords for nothing! I'm trying to tie it up into some sort of meaningful statement!

This is only the beginning. What we're doing won't be too visible for another five years, and then it will be ten years before people realize what's happening and another ten years for people to really get into it. I've got plenty of time. In a sense. Root to the Source gives me even more range than the Art Ensemble. In the Art Ensemble we had to do everything ourselves. Joseph would be the preacher. . . . What you'll see is Root to the Source in combination with the Art Ensemble soon, and then with the addition of a few more horns it'll turn into the Art Ensemble Orchestra with a choir. Soon all these groups are gonna merge on in and do some big things. Because that's our job as musicians, to spread it, we're not supposed to go over in a corner and keep it to ourselves. Take it to Broadway—Root to the Source would be like no other show, structured but different every night—Yankee Stadium. Yeah, that's the only way to do it. Just try to do something big. The way I look at it, most of the time you're broke anyway. No matter what you're doing, you're broke. So you should be doing some big stuff, be broke *for* something. At least you know you've tried. The energy kind of keeps up when you're trying to pull something like that off. At the same time you end up broke. But it's fun and you get things done. We want to have shows and successes, but the main thing we want to do is influence *people*. To make people enjoy life the way we do, and to see it that way, you know, and the beauty and what we can see, the vision that we have. And that's really the main purpose of it, I think that's beneficial. I think that's a nice way to spend your life. And if we can have some broiled shrimp on the way, it's cool!

PRETENDING

Actually I haven't really done shit. Personally, just speaking for myself, I haven't done shit playing no trumpet at all. I can, though, see it coming, like I say, in twenty more years. A little more polish in there. I should be able to play something, I hope, by then, but I've never been satisfied with anything I've done. Everything was done under such *duress*. Take the album *The Great Pretender* (ECM). I think it's going to be a great album, but we did it in two days. Two days and a mix on the third day. Now how can this album—in all kinds of strain! This is between flights. You dig? It isn't like I would get on the phone and say, "Okay, Donald, we're going to rehearse about a month, we're going to research and turn it inside out, then we're going to take another month and make us a really nice album." No, no, I don't get that privilege. It's always. "Okay, you got twenty-four hours." Here's an album that's going to be album of the year, it's gonna win all kinds of awards, its sales are really gonna do something, and I know it ain't shit because it's only a part of what I'm capable of doing. I can only give so much in that situation. Otherwise, if you give too much of your talent, too quickly, you just burn yourself up, you go crazy. So in order to balance it I try to have patience, and meanwhile I just have to go hunting or something. . . . All my records, I've got to sit up here and hope on some stuff I had to rush together, I can't even count on my best work to get me through! That's like developing a whole reputation, and people say, "Lester Bowie, avant-garde trumpet." This is my worst work!

The Great Pretender is an inkling of what Root to the Source might be. It gives you a little idea of the *power* it can have. Root to the Source is an eight-piece band and the *The Great Pretender* is mostly trumpet and rhythm section. One selection on it has got the singers of Root to the Source doing merely some background vocals. It's a little-bitty pinch of what Root to the Source is, and it's probably going to be a smash!

HOW TO PLAY AND WHAT TO WEAR

I feel that the sonoric possibilities of the trumpet have not been fully explored. I think it could be a lot more expressive than what we've been led to believe it can be. I think it's even more vocal than reed instruments. You can get into a baby crying—it's just unbelievable—and I've tried to extend the research in these areas. The trumpet has a certain sound when played so-called correctly, but I've used a lot of different techniques, and some of the sounds seem humorous, but it's not necessarily humor.

People say, "It's an odd sound, so that must mean he has humor in his playing," when actually I'm just extending the sonoric range of the instrument.

In the Art Ensemble we all are in costume, but Roscoe and I don't paint. Because I've always felt that music is like a ceremony. I've always wanted to do something special for that ceremony, even if it's just a hat or a tie, something other than what I would normally be in. Something to transcend the ordinary. Kind of gives you a special feeling. When I put on the white coat it puts me into another whole bag. It's like the African mask. Joseph has a good explanation: the mask serves to eliminate the individual and puts you into the art. That was the purpose of the mask, to take it away from your ordinary being.

I've had all kinds of clown suits, I used to have a whole janitor's outfit, housepainter's outfit when I was painting my house in St. Louis, paint all over it, but I came up on the doctor's thing because it means a couple of things I stand for. Research, for instance. It is a lab jacket, not necessarily a doctor's, that technicians in any field might wear, so it means research when you see it, and I mean research about me playing. I spend a lot of time researching. It's a very scientific approach, and people ask me how is it scientific.

Well, I actually shouldn't even be a trumpet player. I don't have the tooth structure. I've got false teeth. I've got a whole bunch of things that are not natural attributes to playing trumpet. I've had to learn all kinds of tricks to produce what I do because the normal trumpet thing didn't work for me. Sometimes, when I make a move, it's the only way for me to hit the notes. I believe I'm a natural musician but not a natural trumpet player. Maybe I could have been a better saxophone player, a drummer or a bass. So that's why I settle on the lab jacket, and also the fact that it's very easy, something light I can carry around, just one little piece.

You just don't accidentally end up sounding original. You've got to be trying to do it. I found I had to concentrate on developing a specific sound. I'm not a great high-note man. I don't think my technique's going to develop that much more in the future. I may clean up certain things, but mostly work on trying to be personal. Just, you know, make it sound like it's me playing. Because that's the key to the whole thing.

KULCHUR

Like I say, you may find a little storefront museum somewhere in New Orleans or something, but you'll never see a Juilliard School of Music or Philharmonic Hall or anything like that. When you want to research classical music there are libraries you can go to, with volume upon volume, the whole life of Bach, what kind of underwear he wore, everything, all his original manuscripts. But you can't go anywhere and see the Duke's stuff. Well, Duke's stuff may be in the Smithsonian now, but this music isn't—some people have chronicled it, but there are no institutions that really get into it. They just want to get out of it what they can, but they never want to put anything in, which is the shortfall or the downcoming of this country. People are so busy being racist they can't even build a fuel-efficient car.

When you live in a racist country it's weird. Like they'll be so busy being racist against me that I may have the idea that can save the world, or let's say my child has the idea that can save the world, and that child is automatically stopped from getting into it. So you've got all these potential geniuses walking around. You've got musical geniuses in jazz. But these cats end up being winos, end up drinking themselves to death out of frustration. You've got to almost be superhuman. You've got to be Duke Ellington. Or Louis Armstrong. For every Duke Ellington there must've been another thousand cats who wrote well like that. Two or three of them survived, and maybe because their names were "Duke" and "Count." Royalty. That was instrumental. And how many bands were there back in those days? There were a lot.

But that's like part of slavery. You're taught to hate yourself, and after four hundred years it gets to be kind of ingrained. Even genetically. You get to where you feel bad about your color, the way you look. Your eyes or your lips are too big. Your music is not really happening, because first of all they named it "jazz," which means "shit." So you figure it ain't shit because at the time Negroes were property they hated jazz. When I went to Lincoln and you'd try to play some jazz in one of them practice rooms, they'd put you out of school for that. "You play classical!" You're taught to hate yourself.

It would really be something if we had the same budget as, say, the New York Philharmonic. But we can't wait till they decide. We just have to go ahead and get it together. That means getting famous and getting our own money. Shit! If I was a millionaire I would get me enough instruments. Matter of fact, when I go back to Jamaica, when I go back to move, I'm going with enough bread for a house and land, and have enough instruments for a hundred-piece orchestra. I'm going to train everyone in the area for one of the *baddest* bands in the world. The fifty-eight-piece band in New York was the prototype. I would like to have eight hundred just to see what it sounds like. That's what we're developing into once we get this camp going. With 5,800 you could start stations with different elements and you could have different parts synchronized to different notes.

I can organize things. People know it's going to be fun, because that's what usually happens. The Sho' Nuff Orchestra wasn't difficult, because most people want to do something. I could get on the phone and organize another one right now. I've had cats, Jackie McLean for instance, talking to me for the last two years about *volunteering*: "The next time you do anything, like let me know." People *want* to do things.

Maybe I'm crazy. I mean I don't believe this is real, to tell you the truth. I can claim that I'm a heavy, heavy dreamer, but I know how to organize, how to pull them off after I dream them up. I keep on dreaming them, and that always amazes me, so I'm usually pretty happy. I am just amazed that I made it this far, and when I look around I say, *"Damn!"* I didn't ever have a job. I've never been young and frustrated because I've always had my plans. I knew from the beginning that it would take a long time. I wanted to be the number-one jazz trumpeter and I knew it would take twenty years. I know it's going to take another twenty years for what we're talking about now. I'll be sixty then, and then twenty years after that I'll be eighty, and then I'll, you know, white hair, grandchildren all around, but we'll have the camps, and then I'll be getting old, but the camps will be big institutions, temples and shit. I got it figured that I'm going to live until I'm ninety-six, and by then this shit will be really big. And I'll have a big hip funeral. Big.

It will be world music by then.

We are talking about the Art Ensemble of Mexico.

LESTER BOWIE'S EQUIPMENT

I've got a Benge trumpet. For the first time I've been given horns. The Benge company gave me this set of horns. I've always played a custom-made trumpet. This one's called a Claude Gordon model. I used to play a Shilke trumpet for eleven years. I still use a Shilke mouthpiece.

—June 1982

CHARLIE HADEN

BY RAFI ZABOR

■

The radio crackles in

1939. . . . KMA, 50,000 watts out of Shenandoah, Iowa:

Keep on the sunny side of life

Keep on the sunny side of life

Keep on the sunny side

Always on the sunny side

Keep on the sunny side of life

"All right, kiddies; thanks, friends; it's the Haden

children, Carl Junior, Mary Elizabeth, little Jimmy,

and little two-year-old Charlie, entertaining on the reglar nine-thirty progrum this morning. Now then, I want to say thanks to each and every one of you good friends who have sent in orders for the youngsters' pictures, who have written in those fine cards and letters, we do appreciate the nice things you have to say about our kiddies. I also want to thank you men who have written in to 'Opportunity' and let me say to more of you, if you men are looking for bigger and better-paying jobs, here's one business, friends, that needs more men and they need 'em now. It's the air-conditioning and refrigeration industry. In every community there is a growing demand for men trained in the planning, installation, and servicing of refrigeration and air-conditioning equipment. Now to train your men, mechanically minded between eighteen and fifty . . ."

Is that your father?

That's him. Let me move the tape ahead.

"Now, on with the progrum. More dedications this morning. We're gonna have little two-year old Charlie up here now, to sing a song for you and to yodel for you this morning, and Charlie's got numbers picked out that he's been request, and we want to do these numbers for Mr. and Mrs. Leon Paber of Kellogg, Iowa, for their little son Delvin's second birthday, for Mrs. Jake Gardner of Omaha, Nebraska, for grandson Charles Edward Bronson's second birthday, for Bobby Taylor, Evelyn Ingram, Darlene Ingram and Kenneth Dobbs, and Mrs. W. W. Kibbler, this is the Golden Rule Sunday School class who are listening in this morning, what do you think of that? That's fine and dandy, we're mighty happy to hear from all you good friends, and now then little two-year-old Charles Edward, we believe to be the youngest cowboy singer and yodeler on the air, is gonna sing a verse of the song 'The Birmingham Jail.' All right, honey."

Down in the valley, valley so low
Hang your head over, hear the wind blow. . . .

Were you under any pressure to join the show?

Oh, no. When my mother used to rock me to sleep, she would sing—she had a fantastic voice, like Joan Baez—and I would hum along with her. She saw that I liked it and I got older she started teaching me the words to songs and I was there, in her arms, when they did the shows. She was a great singer, and still is. She sang all the great folk songs—"Barbara Allen," "Mansion on the Hill," "Wildwood Flower"—and my father was one of the greatest harmonica players I ever heard. He could improvise and all my brothers and sisters were good musicians and they sang really true.

"And now for a song and a yodel. He's gonna sing a song about his old dog, Shep. 'Old Shep,' a song and a yodel. All right, Charlie. . . ."

When I was a lad and old Shep was a pup. . . .

The house was full of sponsors' products. Sparkalite Cereal. Cocoa-Wheats with vitamin G. Green Mountain Cough Syrup. We had crates of the stuff. When I was five, my father bought a farm outside of Springfield, Missouri—I was raised in Springfield mostly. The radio studio was right in the house. I'd wake up, watch my family go out to milk the cows, watch them come back in. We'd eat breakfast and then do the radio show, every day but Sunday, fifteen minutes to half an hour. This was during the war. Later my father tired of the farm and bought a restaurant. That time the studio was upstairs.

All those songs we used to sing were very beautiful, and they've stayed with me. Some of them come back to me even now. I started improvising folk songs when I did the *80/81* album with Pat Metheny and recently when I was playing with Denny Zeitlin in San Francisco we played something that made me remember all these things. What I want to do now is stop in Missouri on my way back to Los Angeles and spend some time with my mom and this time get some songs from her. I want to relearn them. Because it's really important music. It comes through this country from Europe but most people, when they think of the only art form in American music, think of jazz. I grew up knowing Mother Maybelle Carter. Some of the best music I've ever heard was Maybelle Carter playing guitar and singing, and A. P. Carter and her sister, and the Delmore Brothers singing. . . . Oh, man, they were fantastic. I saw a special view of country America that you don't get in the city. I used to go to houses in rural Missouri and people would be on their porches singing and playing fiddles and blowing into moonshine jugs, playing washboards and spoons. My grandpa used to play the fiddle held under his chest instead of his chin, and he used to tell me stories about Frank and Jesse James, the Younger brothers and the Daltons. My grandma told me about Wild Bill Hickock in Springfield, Missouri.

We used to play a lot of revival meetings and tent meetings and county fairs on truck beds—we'd be standing on flatbed trucks at fairgrounds, and at racetracks we'd be on the grandstand performing. We traveled all over the Midwest doing that when I was a kid. I was very small the first time my parents took me to a black church to hear the music, I couldn't believe it, I just sat there and listened. I couldn't believe how beautiful it was and I didn't want to leave. I just wanted to stay.

I was raised in a place that forced you into political awareness early, seeing racism all around you. In the county where I graduated high school, blacks weren't allowed to remain in the county after dark—this was 1955. There was only one movie theater they could go to, and they had to sit in the third balcony.

I sang with the family until I was fifteen, when I had bulbar polio. I caught it when we were doing a television show in Omaha during an epidemic. The doctor said I was lucky—it hit the nerve to my face and throat and vocal cords, and it usually hits the legs and lungs. It took about a year for the effects to go away and after that I couldn't really sing, couldn't control the note and hold vibrato.

I started playing bass when I was fourteen. I've always felt the bass was beautiful. I loved the sound of it. When I sang, I always wanted to sing the bass part even though my voice wasn't low enough. I was attracted to it more than to any other instrument. When I was in grade school, my brother Jim, who was the bass player on our show, was interested in jazz. Jim started bringing home Jazz at the Philharmonic records and Lionel Hampton, Dizzy Gillespie, Billie Holiday, Stan Kenton. I didn't know what it was, didn't know what improvising meant, I just knew that I loved the way it sounded. And the more I heard it the more I loved it—the harmonies, the voicings, the textures and the chords, and the first chance I got, I went to a concert. I was fourteen and we were in Omaha. My family was up there doing a television show every week and Jazz at the Philharmonic came through and I went with some friends. Charlie Parker was playing, and Lester Young and Flip Philips, Willie the Lion Smith, Roy Eldridge, Oscar Peterson, Ray Brown, and it was really something.

When we moved back to Springfield, Stan Kenton's band came through. Dan Bagley was playing bass and Stan Levey drums. I went backstage and talked to them. They invited me up to their hotel. They were impressed that I was so young, in such a small town in the Midwest, and wanted to play jazz. I asked them where I should go, New

York or Los Angeles, and most of them, their advice was: Don't play music, don't play jazz, it's a rough life; you have to go on the road and you can't have a family. But I kept after them and Don Bagley told me who he was studying with in L.A. When Kenton came back next time, Max Bennett was on bass, Mel Lewis played drums and Charlie Mariano was in the band. After the concert, I went to a jam session in somebody's house and I got to play. Before that, I had just been playing with records.

Then there was a TV show that came to Springfield from Nashville called "The Ozark Jubilee." Red Foley was the star, and Eddie Arnold used to come up and he brought Hank Garland with him—he was a great jazz guitar player—and I played in that show with Grady Martin, a guitarist with Red Foley, and the pianist with Grady was a jazz player. I found out from him that a lot of players from Nashville really love jazz. Sometimes we would jam. Grady Martin played Bob Wills–style, Western swing, sort of, but what I tried to get them to do was play Bird tunes and bebop. That was mostly my experience in Springfield. In high school, I didn't have many close friends. Most of the guys in my class were involved in Future Farmers of America. I used to bring them to my house to listen to Bird and they'd look at me like I was some kind of . . .

I was playing completely by ear, which is one thing I think that caused me to be introverted, shy, and soft-spoken. I felt that I didn't know enough about music, that I was inferior to the musicians I was playing with, though on the radio we had to be perfect, you know, you couldn't be sharp or flat. I applied to Oberlin and got a full scholarship even though I was completely self-taught, but then I heard about Westlake College of Modern Music, which was like Berklee and had a good reputation for jazz studies. I turned down the scholarship, sold shoes until I made seven hundred and fifty dollars, said good-bye to my parents, got on a Greyhound with a suitcase and my plywood Kay bass, and went straight through to L.A. The people from Westlake met me at the bus station. I lived in a dorm off Sunset and though Westlake had a few good teachers I became disenchanted with the place. I met a lot of musicians right away and started working. I met Red Mitchell in a coffee shop at three in the morning—I had listened to him and Hampton Hawes on records—and we played together at his house. One day he had a record date and couldn't make a gig with Art Pepper. I covered for him and Art hired me for the rest of the gig.

The reason I'm talking about my past is to convey my need to know how people who dedicate their lives to an art form grow up, what happens to them. I would like to know what happened to Django. I'd like to know about Bach's childhood.

My father lived until 1974. He was sixty-four. We were really close. In the late sixties when I was about thirty, I had a dream that I was on an old-fashioned train. It was 1939 in the dream but I was still thirty years old—and 1939 was the year my father was thirty. The conductor came through and said, "Shenandoah, next stop." I got off the train and there was an old train-depot newsstand. Everything cost a nickel or three pennies. I went into a phone booth and looked up our name, and there was my father's name and the street we lived on. I wanted to call him, but I was afraid, so I walked out onto the street. Old cars were going by, and our car passed, our old Oldsmobile. My father was driving, and my mother was holding me, and I was asleep, a two-year-old boy. My brothers and sisters were playing in the backseat. I went into a restaurant feeling like the wind was knocked out of me, and I asked the guy behind the counter if he knew Carl Haden. He said, "Everybody knows Carl Haden. The Hadens are on the radio here every morning." I told the guy I wanted to talk to Carl and he said, "if you want to see him come down here, I know a good way. He's a harmonica fanatic, so tell him you got some new harps for sale and he'll come."

I went to the phone, put a nickel in and dialed the number. My father answered, I said hello and he said, "Who's this?" I said, "Well, I'm in town and I've got some harmonicas for sale and I heard you might be interested." He said, "I'll be right down."

I waited. I didn't know what to do. And in a few minutes, he came in. And, man, that was worth the whole dream, just to see him. He had all his hair and he wasn't gray. He was young. He had a pin-striped suit with a tie and one of those round collars. It was just unbelievable to see him. I was his age. We just stood and looked at each other. I wanted to say, "I'm your son!" But I didn't. We shook hands, and went to sit down in one of the booths. I stared at him. He stared at me and said, *"Haven't I seen you somewhere before?"* Then I woke up. That dream came out a real yearning. I had always wanted to be able to talk to my father and be the same age as he was. I had the dream while he was still alive, and I always wanted to tell him about it, but I never had the chance. Maybe I was afraid to tell him—now this is really strange—because he would have remembered the day that somebody called him down to the depot.

How did you meet Ornette Coleman?

I was playing with a lot of people in L.A., and the more I played standards the more dissatisfied I became. Especially when I played solos. Even lines behind a musician—I wasn't satisfied with the normal, traditional way of playing chord changes. Little by little I started trying to play what I was hearing. Say I would be soloing on "All the Things You Are," and maybe there was a group of notes I wanted to play off of, or a phrase from somebody's solo, or I wanted to play on the melody instead of the changes. And I tried but it was hard, because I had never tried to express it before. Musicians would get upset because they wouldn't know where I was in the song or when to come back in.

Then one night I was at a club called the Hague—I think I was listening to Gerry Mulligan's group—and all of a sudden this guy gets up on stage with a plastic alto and starts playing, and the creative energy level changed completely—it was going through the ceiling, it was the most brilliant sound I'd ever heard and I said, "Who is that? Who is that man?" Someone said, "That's Ornette Coleman." I wanted to meet him. By the time I got behind the bandstand to meet him they had already asked him to stop playing and he had disappeared out the back door. But Lenny McBrowne told me how to find him.

I went to Ornette's house and told him I'd heard him play the other night and that it was beautiful, and he said thanks, because he wasn't used to hearing someone say that to him, and the first time we played, I found myself able to play what I'd been hearing, though I did do some struggling. It was like jumping into a pool or a creek you've never been in before—there were growing pains, trying to find which notes sounded good against what he was playing. Experiencing a fear of something different than any other experience I'd ever had, and he had that clear, natural, beautiful sound. It was like no other music in the world. This was in 1957.

I'd actually met Don Cherry and Billy Higgins before Ornette. We got together and started playing at Don Cherry's house. We would play every day and stop and talk about what we were doing and then we would play the tune over again. It was really something.

Coming to New York in 1959 was really exciting. I'd never been there before, and after checking into the hotel we went down to the Five Spot for a rehearsal and I had never seen anything like that before, derelicts lying there on the street. I started to bend down to help one guy and one of the other musicians who was playing the Five Spot said, "What are you doing?" The guy's lying on the sidewalk! "Hey man, you're in New York City! You can't help that, man!" When we started playing every night, the place was packed with people not just from the music world but from the art world, from everywhere. There were famous painters, poets. One night I was playing—you know, I usually play with my eyes closed—and I happened to open my eyes and looked down and there was Leonard Bernstein with his ear next to my bass, right on the bandstand. He asked me where I'd studied and I told him I was self-taught and he couldn't believe that. He invited me to come up to the Philharmonic, and years later, when I was sure he had forgotten me, he was of tremendous help to me with the Guggenheim Foundation, when I applied for a fellowship in composition.

One night we were playing, Cherry was taking a solo and all of a sudden I heard the solo change direction and I opened my eyes and it was Miles. He had gotten up on the stand, taken Cherry's horn and started playing. And there wasn't a night when I didn't open my eyes, look out at the audience or the bar and see some great bass player checking me out. Paul Chambers, Percy Heath, Mingus. Those were exciting days. Then we went on the road and scared everybody to death in the towns we played—Boston, Chicago, Pittsburgh, Philadelphia. The musicians would come to hear us, word had come down the grapevine, people were expecting something new.

It made a lot of musicians angry, not so much angry as insecure. People had been conditioned to a certain way of hearing music, and if they had to stop and think, or use their senses in a new way they got insecure. You don't think about sensitive musicians doing it, but with our music it was like that. It was so different, a different way of approaching the language of jazz that it pressed a lot of people's buttons, and fights broke out, I mean real fistfights broke out in the Five Spot, people arguing about if we knew what we were doing—we did vs. we didn't—then all kinds of insults were shouted, then *bam bam bam* and cars were set on fire and someone came into the Five Spot one night and hit Ornette. . . . When we were interviewed, people asked us how all the controversy affected us. I answered that we didn't have time to be affected by it. We were thinking about playing, and trying to figure out other ways to play what we were hearing. Each time we played, the more sure we became what we were doing and the more we knew that it was important to play. Our way of improvising was unique—like another language. There aren't that many people who have experienced it; just a handful of them, and all of them come through Ornette's band— Dewey, Don Cherry, Billy Higgins, Eddie Blackwell, Bobby Bradford.

Coltrane used to come in and listen, wait for us to finish and then go out with Ornette and talk for hours. He was looking for a way to play what he was hearing, looking for different kinds of solutions, remedies or methods. One of the things he wanted to find out was what it was like to play with our band. He had this record date and he called Blackwell and Cherry and me to play with him. It was a great experience but I didn't know what he expected of us at first. Gradually I found out he wanted us to play as we did with Ornette. We recorded a lot that day, some of which isn't on the album *(The Avant Garde)*.

Then Sonny Rollins hired Don and Billy, and I was supposed to be on that band, too, but I was incapacitated. I remember Cherry calling me up to go with them to Europe. Actually I left Ornette's band to go to Lexington Public Health Service Hospital—that was in 1960, and when I got back to New York we made the double-quartet record *(Free*

Jazz)—I was uncomfortable on that because I had to play a borrowed bass and it wasn't that great an instrument—and then I got arrested in New York, lost my cabaret card, got put on probation, broke probation, left for Los Angeles. I rejoined Ornette in 1966 when I got my health back. I had been to Synanon. From 1963 to 1973 I was clean. I don't like to talk about heroin addiction because that tends to romanticize the situation. One thing I do know, drugs will not help a mediocre musician sound better and the great musicians I've known who happened to be addicted played great in spite of their addition, not because of it. When I stopped using chemicals, my music became much stronger. It is important for me to stay healthy, not only for my sake, but for my children's. They ought to have someone to look up to. I'm not proud of any of this. If I hadn't kicked, I would have died, and that's that.

For a frightening picture of Haden as dying young junkie, see the cover of Ornette Coleman's *This Is Our Music*; for what he had accomplished so young (he has since accomplished a good deal more), try listening to contents of same. What he worked out early on, in a band, remember, that revolutionized the art of jazz in our time, is a modal style sprung freely enough to accommodate Coleman's untempered sense of pitch and unorthodox departures from diatonic tonality, a beat wide enough to unlock the gates of the bar lines when necessary, and most of all a depth of feeling capable of real response to Coleman's unforgettable, mother-naked utterance; but when I think of Charlie Haden I don't call to mind his *Contribution to the Art of Modern Bass*, which is formidable, but (for example) the image of him standing onstage with Pat Metheny's *80/81* band two years back at the Joyous Lake in Woodstock, his bass accompaniment rising like sap through the tree of a Metheny solo and then opening nave, transepts, arches, galleries, towers, and aisles in chorus after chorus of Dewey Redman tenor while light fell in shafts from the windows and Metheny sat there on his stool in this sudden cathedral, shook his head and stared. It was a kind of playing, a kind of getting into the substance of someone else's music that goes well beyond "he's got great ears" to recall Rilke's notion of two solitudes growing so large and deep they can include each other, an encounter of whole and unfalsified individualities unhampered by the passing chords of space and time.

But then I could have called to mind other equally articulate moments, like Haden one night on a Boston stage with Old and New Dreams playing a solo in which he questioned his notes so deeply it seemed as if at any moment they might fess up and tell him the meaning of his life. The moment produced an inconceivable hush in the hall as Haden drew us so powerfully into his world it became identical to our own. We sat there, having paid seven-fifty for our tickets, at one of the limits of music, where sound was about to give out and a world of unmeasured Meaning, from which music derives and at which it is always pointing back, was about to burst through the stable look of things and, finally, speak.

Everyone knows there are two schools of bass playing, the Fast and the Slow (that's a *joke*, Charlie); Haden has taken the Slow and made it into an extraordinary instrument of self-exploration. I think of him as having made himself over the years, through a mix of inspiration and catastrophe, into the kind of musician whose work attracts to itself inevitable metaphysical weight: he has intuited something central to himself as man and musician and gone forward towards it by the stripping away of successive surfaces so that you hear, in addition to the human turnings of the music through the volutions of his identity, every vibration of string, every creak and strain of wood, the labor of brain, heart and fingers in a concentrated pursuit of final essences, a consciously impassioned hunt for the ultimately real. You might object that good jazz musicians do this all the time—it's certainly true that if you listen to Johnny Hodges right he'll peel you like a grape—but the process is made so plain in Haden that he becomes an object lesson in how such a quest might be carried out and what you are likely to find along the way. I think it's important that what Haden finds is not merely, as so many do these days at the played-out end of Western Sievelization, reality deconstructed into its unappetizing and useless components (which then are either left lying around or get hustled into forms as rigid as they are arbitrary) but Truth, Beauty, Dignity and all the fine old things, and the point about Haden is that he gets it all into the music with no tricky bits missing and no lies told along the way and you believe him. And to me, at any rate, that's important.

Ideal though Haden was in the early days with the classic Coleman quartet—have you noticed how much more perfect the records have gotten over the years?—Haden didn't come into the full range of his voice until a few years later. Judging purely by the recorded evidence and my own awakening to him when he played in Berkeley, California, with Ornette, he certainly had it together by 1970. The bassist who plays on Ornette's *Science Fiction, Broken Shadows* and *Friends and Neighbors,* his own *Liberation Music Orchestra,* and the overture to Carla Bley's *Escalator Over the Hill* (a remarkable solo over unprecedented accompaniment) had evolved dramatically since the early sixties. His time, although it had strengthened audibly between 1959 and '60, had greater personal authority now, and he had developed a number of original devices for work in the rhythm section of which perhaps the most powerful was a multistringed drone that he could pivot up or down as if on pedal point—the sound itself is enormous, like a choir of basses, and the effect behind a soloist is stunning, as if Haden were enlarging to the point of explosion the harmonic implications of the solo line while at the same time creating maximum tension between the drummer's timekeeping and his own. It's worth pointing out how technically similar to, but sonically different from, guitar and banjo picking patterns this is, because it shows to what personal uses the mature Haden could put his country heritage. Although a certain amount of guitaristic strumming was common to the bass playing of the period—Haden's own solo figure for Coleman's "Ramblin'" providing one example—Haden's later appropriation of fingerpicking patterns sound almost nothing like their source, the kind of appropriation only master musicians seem able to manage. Country music also shows up in the sometime surprisingly simple resolutions dramatically attenuated melodies in his bass solos will come to. Just the other day, I put on *Liberation Music Orchestra* and listened to Haden's accompaniment to Carla Bley's piano solo on "War Orphans." His probing triplet figures were so beautiful a way of playing a love duet with Carla, and so perfect an expression of the nature of the bass, it took me a while to realize that nobody had played the instrument like that until Haden came along and did it. He is by now so familiar a part of modern bass playing that you can paradoxically forget how original he is.

As a soloist the mature Haden evolved an eloquent solo style that ran counter to the practices of most of his contemporaries. While virtually everyone else sought to deemphasize the difficulty of the instrument and to demonstrate that the acoustic bass could be played as fluently, and in some hands as quickly, as a horn, Haden, in his note choices, minute variations of pitch, fingering and tone, seemed almost to go out of his way to encounter obstructions to a facilely flowing solo line and the superficial resolutions of a conventionally masterful technique, as if to say, "There's a lot more to life than *that*." He arrives at an expression of beauty in which the distances traveled and the price paid are part of the statement.

Chronology, ontogeny, pharmacology. In the seventies he worked most famously with Keith Jarrett; with Ornette on the rare occasions the latter was willing to appear, with Ornette's alumni in Old and New Dreams (one of this period's classic bands); struggled to reunite the Liberation Music Orchestra. His wife Ellen gave birth to a son, Josh, in '68; triplets (Rachel, Petra, Tanya) in '71; blessings which must somehow be paid for on a musician's income. Haden had been making major music for some time. Finally, in 1977 he released the breathtaking *Closeness*, the first of a series of albums of duets that should have accorded him career-making recognition at last. But a series of traumas started him using again and he entered the Delancey Street Foundation in San Francisco to kick, shaved his head, surrendered his bass, mopped floors, answered the switchboard, raised funds. Two years of his life . . . some people have all the luck.

But let's talk about duets. "I could do duets for the next twenty years. When I think of all the great musicians I haven't played duets with, I could play duets for the rest of my life."

Well, yes. And it's even obvious why. For a bassist with fabulous ears and an eerie way of inhabiting other people's music—and think for a minute what it might be like to play with him as he articulates things in your music you yourself didn't know were there, as if he could find the universal hidden in any particular and bring it out to show—it must be quite a pleasure to intensify your listening one-on-one, unobscured by the racket of cymbals and drums; for Haden is obsessed with communication as only someone whose music speaks out of an extraordinary degree of solitude can be, and his solitude is as pronounced, beautiful, and dangerous as any musician's, even unto Miles. When he speaks of things important to him (you should know before going on), Haden's voice takes on some of the pauses and the quavering intensity of his bass playing. It's the voice, perhaps, of someone who has been broken to pieces past all repair and then, unexpectedly reconstructed, became unable to take anything for granted again, though his polio-constricted throat keeps the pitch medium high. One of the most important parts of the creative process in improvised music is listening, and when just two people are playing you can listen so much more clearly. My focusing when I write or play is on the other people involved, not on myself, and that's in my mind the whole time I'm working, to make the musician feel so good in what he's doing that he's able to express himself to his very highest potential. I usually know the musicians well and am inspired by them, and that makes it easy. And if I'm writing something inspired by a particular person or place, that enters into it. And then I have the listener in mind. The only time I come into it is when I'm playing, but when you're in the midst of creating and are close to music, that goes, too.

Have you ever found yourself getting in the way because the music's going especially badly or especially well?

When I have trouble with that, it means I'm not involved in my work. I want to be able to rise above my own self-needs more and more, to be able to give to others and have concern for others and to rise above that ego, and I hope that other people will be able to do that, too. Did you see the notes from Hamp's album, *As Long as There's Music*? One of the things I said in that, although it might seem idealistic, was that in every human being there is a godlike quality that is creative. Every human being, when they're born, when they're a child, has potentially endless possibilities inside themselves, and one of these is creative expression. With a lot of people, as they grow up, it gets stifled or taken away, and I want them to know that they have that inside them, and that they can discover it and nourish it and let it come out. And as long as there's music there will be a way for people to discover that quality inside them. When I'm making a record, when I know someone is going to listen to that record, I think about the reality of their lives and the reality of them listening to it, and I want to be able to capture them, even if it's only for a moment, and I want that moment to be as complete and honest as it possibly can. Because it's difficult for people, even when they're having conversations with each other, to listen to each other, but I've met some people in my life who really know how to listen and it's fantastic. When I write or play something and one of my children likes it, that's also very meaningful to me, because their response is genuine and immediate. The world may be lost as far as the adults are concerned. I think we have to teach children and surround them with creative thought and show them how precious life is and how we have to use intelligence to enhance it, not just for our own good. That's one of the responsibilities of an artist.

People ask me what I think about when I'm improvising, and I have to tell them there's no thought process. You have to get to know music as you would a person, and get close to music as you would to a friend, and the closer you get, the nearer you are to touching music, and when you're really playing, when you're really touching music, if you try to remember back you'll see that your ears become your mind, your feelings become your mind, and there is no thought process as far as the intellect is concerned. It's coming from the emotions and from whatever energy is passing from the music to you. The ego goes away. Or should I say, you reach a place where there is no ego, and in doing that you see yourself in relation to the rest of the universe, and you see your unimportance in relation to the rest of the universe, and in seeing your unimportance you begin to see your importance. You see that it's important to have respect and reverence for life and music, and in being able to do that you get close to being honest in your playing. When someone says, "He plays great," that's what you're doing, playing honestly. And striving for beauty. When you think about inspiration it's startling, because there really are no words there. And the communication shouldn't *stop* with music. You should go on from there.

Have you changed, then? Have you begun to see this in explicitly mystical terms?

I'm interested in reading and learning about different religions from different cultures, but for myself I feel a strong need for self-reliance and for believing in something I feel close to, which is Life. It's very difficult for me to use a word that's used by hypocrites, and that's why I don't use the word God very much. That's been misused in many languages by people who are not worthy of using the word, I don't like to think of myself as having to depend on anyone else or follow anyone else in order to discover the essence of life. That's a constant discovery that never ends, and I think a guru or someone like that can be very dangerous to rely on.

You do have a strong sense of the sacred, of the sacredness of things.

I believe that the sacred is in the ordinary. As Maslow said, people spend their whole lives in search for the exotic, the strange, the mystical, and in the end find that the sacred is in the ordinary: in one's backyard, family, friends. I believe that a great man is like that guy who saved that stewardess in that plane crash in Washington. He jumped into that icy water without even thinking about it, and the quality inside that man, that's godlike to me, that's greatness to me. He didn't want to be interviewed about it, he didn't want to talk about it, he just wanted to go back to work. That quality I can admire, giving in an unselfish way.

Let's talk about the Liberation Music Orchestra. Granted that the political state of the world is horrific at the moment, what can you hope to accomplish with the Orchestra?

I'm not a politician. I'm a human being trying to learn about this life, and I'm a musician. But I want to play this music, to find music from different parts of the world that has to do with people fighting for their right to live freely. The music that comes from that struggle should be heard by as many people as possible. That music also inspires people to play their best, and I want to be able to inform people in a real way about what's happening in the world, the struggle in El Salvador, in Chile, in Nicaragua. We sit here in the United States and watch it on television and lose touch with the reality and I feel a responsibility to communicate my feelings in an honest way to as many people as I can, and if I can change just one person's outlook, then I feel like I've accomplished something. We're in a dangerous situation. Nuclear war is a real possibility, and "The Day After," although good, was a lightweight Hollywood soap-opera version. You can see that Reagan's a figurehead, that he uses his ability as an actor to make everyone go for the invasion of Grenada, for the contras in Nicaragua, for the death squads in El Salvador. . . . And both Kennedys are gone, Martin Luther King, Malcolm X, Allende. . . .

Do you think the left-wing revolutions have worked out all that well?

No. In most cases they haven't. I don't know what happened. If the leaders of the governments of the world were able to hear—I know this is very idealistic—if they were able to hear the beauty of the slow movement of Shostakovich's *Fifth Symphony*, or Ravel, or Richard Strauss's *Four*

Last Songs, or Canteloube's *Songs of the Auvergne*, or Billie
Holiday, Django Reinhardt, Charlie Parker, Bill Evans, Ornette Coleman . . . if they could really hear the beauty. . . .
Sometimes I think about hearing music through someone
else's ears and it frightens me—if someone wanted to tor-
ture me, they could force me to hear music through Ronald
Reagan's ears. He must be *tone-deaf.* When you think about
composers and painters who try to change the world with
their art form, you wonder what it would be like if people
like them governed the world. But, especially in America,
intelligent people are not attracted to politics. When I hear
great music I think that musician, that person, must have
so much love inside. When I spoke earlier about improvisation, of seeing your own importance—when you're playing
in the moment—experiencing the moment, it shows you
the brilliance in the universe, and that brilliance is in every
human being. If the people who run the governments of
the world could touch that brilliance inside themselves,
and know that it's in everyone else and everywhere else,
the world just couldn't go on the same way, the way it's
going now.

The week of this last recorded talk, I managed to hear
Haden twice with the New York edition of the Liberation
Music Orchestra—there's another one in Los Angeles—at
Seventh Avenue South, a small room that the twelve-piece
band filled with music of tremendous and audible human-
ity. As Haden said, the material from Spain and Latin
America was so packed with its own meanings and pas-
sions that the soloists were inspired to surpass themselves.
I heard particularly stunning work from Dewey Redman,
Baikida Carroll, Amina Claudine Myers and Craig Harris;
Carroll told me later that the simple music, full of unfake-
able feeling, inspired him in one direction and the fast
modernist company with its own unfakeabilities inspired

him in another, which seems as good a definition of the band's working amplitude of expression as you're likely to get. The band's performance style was a lot closer to the epochal abandon of the 1970 unit than to the tidier and more stoical temper of the recent record, *Ballad of the Fallen*, on ECM, and if the LMO does succeed in getting its bulk out on the road as planned, I expect it to shake significant portions of the American superflux and establish itself as one of the indispensable bands of the period.

As for Haden, he sounded like a whole orchestra of basses, with an orchestra's repertoire of sonic resource: countermelodies over varying drones, pluckings and strummings, extended radical gambits, insupportable tensions, all four strings going at once—Haden's is nothing if not a virtuoso approach to the instrument, a high-wire act on four strings. It's paradoxical, though not really surprising if you take Haden's remarks on the evanescence of the self as prelude to the emergence of the real as seriously as I do, that a musician who habitually talks of his work in abnegatory terms—of others rather than himself, of listening instead of playing, effacement rather than expansion, even of drummers "so good they're bassists and I don't even have to play"—should, more than any other bassist playing today and probably more than any bassist since Mingus, determine the coloration of any band he plays with. Add him to or subtract him from any band you can convince to play in your mind: he has learned to make an unforgettable mark.

His plans for the future include Japanese and American tours for the New York edition of the Liberation Music Orchestra (Haden also intends to incorporate new material into its repertoire), tours and an album with Old and New Dreams, a solo bass album for ECM based on folk tunes collected by his mother, possibly another album for solo bass and string orchestra, a project with Herbie Hancock, a trio album with Pat Metheny and Billy Higgins already in the can at ECM, and something/anything with Ornette Coleman, with whom Haden plays when he's in New York and who tells Haden he's ready to do something any time. Currently Haden is living in Los Angeles to be near his kids and teaching jazz improvisation at Cal Arts. When his children are older, he expects to move back to New York to be nearer the music.

Whatever he does, I expect to be there listening, and I expect it to be as important to me as it's been until now. As usual, it's a damn shame that jazz is such a minority music, because what Haden's got to say is of use to anyone out there trying to learn what is to be human. He is one of those artists through whom the brilliance of the universe is made more articulate and manifest, and this is a liberation from which others necessarily follow. Keep on the sunny side of life, Charlie. Keep on the sunny side of life.

—April 1984

Wynton Vs. Herbie:

The Purist and

the Crossbreeder

Duke It Out

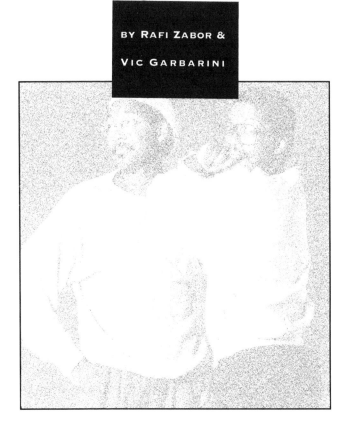

By Rafi Zabor & Vic Garbarini

■

You can see how it was sup-
posed to work. Take The Brilliant Young Trumpeter
Wynton Marsalis, who has taken some time out from
his precocious and dramatic ascent to denounce the
commercial moves of certain of his elders, and sit him
down with The Great and Distinguished Pianist Herbie Hancock, who among Marsalis's significant elders
has made the most undilutedly commercial moves, ask
them a handful of questions, and wait for either an
interesting discussion or sparks. The two musicians

have played together—in fact, Hancock gave Marsalis a portentous boost early in his development by touring with him and producing his first record—respect each other's abilities even if they disagree mightily about matters of aesthetic choice, and both record for Columbia, the gem of the ocean. So pass me a Thracian sword and a Scythian axe, honey, and meet me at Black Rock.

We met twelve stories up a black obelisk in a republic that was preparing to reelect Ronald Reagan as its President. Despite these looming omens, we began by assuring each other of our degree of mutual culture: the critics told the musicians that the last thing they wanted to provoke was an argument, and the musicians told the critics that an argument between them could not possibly be provoked. Then we all proceeded to behave unpredictably. Herbie Hancock laid out, much as he had during the horn solos in his middle years with the Miles Davis Quintet, and Wynton Marsalis, whose early phrasing suggested an altogether charming if equally deceptive shyness, was off on a long and continuously impressive solo. Aggressive? Well, yes, you could call it that.

His fulmination against the concept of "soul" stands most in need of introduction. A couple of days after the interview, however, Marsalis filled in some of the blanks at the Bottom Line after his band's last set.

What bothered him about the notion of soul as conventionally applied is the racist subtext: black musicians are expected to be "soulful" and inarticulate, to perpetuate the myth of the gifted primitive whose sources of inspiration are racial and mysterious and therefore *not his own*, which is to say he is not a conscious artist in the deific Western sense of the term, and even if a genius, automatically one of the second rank. What's worse, he went on, is that some black people, writers among them, internalize the discrimination and identify rootsiness with lack of knowledge.

Young musicians tell Marsalis that they want to learn their music from the street, which, of course, is to stay precisely where the wheel of history has put you and say that you've begun to like it. Marsalis's personal reversal of the stereotype is deliberate and organic and, if you consider his conquest of the classical music world, quite graphic. Likewise the way he deals with, ahem, critics. Not content to issue contemptuous one-liners in the Miles Davis tradition, Marsalis actually *remembers* what his critics write about him— probably the first time anyone anywhere has actually bothered to do this—and is willing to confront them, in person or in print, with the concrete evidence of their musical illiteracy. Since (as is widely known) critics know even less about music than they do about writing and since Marsalis's conceptual and verbal apparati are in excellent trim, the job is easily done. On the other hand, his habitual distaste for the press can lead to aggressive and unintentionally provocative interviews, as occasionally here.

A backstage visit to the Bottom Line illustrated another side of the media coin. As I came in, Marsalis was handing round the last of many glasses of champagne to a large group of friends, when someone called him a star. Wynton ducked and said, *"Don't call me that.* Call me that and I'll never get a good review again." Which brings us to the subject of Marsalismania and its attendant backlash.

I remember walking up and down a ticket line for an Art Ensemble concert a couple of months back and, honest, it seemed that Wynton Marsalis was the only topic of conversation. "Cold." "No feeling." "A technician." "A light-skinned Negro who plays classical music." "Wears suits." "Behaves." Other voices, probably a musician's: "I hope he's puttin' some money away while this is happening because, man, this can't last." Of course, some of the hostility he's picking up is actually directed at Columbia Records, whose faithless and hubristic way of proclaiming and then discarding jazz stars is widely disliked. For Wynton Marsalis is not only the finest straightahead trumpeter to turn up in the last couple of decades, he is, in a culture that usually doesn't care whether its jazz musicians live or die, a genuine phee-nomenon. Maybe it's the classical connection, or maybe it's the suits, but *Think of One* reportedly sold 200,000 copies, the string album, *Hot House Flowers*, has a chance of selling half a million and going gold, and cousins of mine who never bought a jazz record in their lives have begun to ask me if he's the real thing. And this drives the hipsters mad, insofar as a portion of the jazz audience defines itself by listening to music that no one else wants to hear.

I like Marsalis's two new albums better than most of my friends and neighbors. I'm not wild about the string charts on *Hot House Flowers*, although they are more imaginative than they have to be to satisfy the demands of genre—and I appreciate Wynton's tact in not taking all the solos for himself. But what thrills me on the record are three or four of the trumpet solos. Those old-fashioned chord changes take off some of the chill that the recording process seems to impart to Marsalis's work. One thing I've always admired in his work is the instinctive flex of note against note in his phrasing, the uncoiling of his solos in compelling patterns of tension and release that get your attention and hold it for the distance even if the solo is short on organization after its first couple of choruses. But on the new album, most spectacularly on "When You Wish Upon a Star" but even more convincingly on "I'm Confessin'," there is something more, the kind of form that can only evolve organically, and at a significant spiritual depth. It's true that his work on this album still leans on late-fifties Miles Davis—but no more, say, than Clifford Brown did on Fats Navarro. So there. As for the classical album, a mostly Purcell affair with Edita Grugerova, I know that people have expressed their disappointment at the too-miscellaneous nature of the repertoire, but why has no one pointed out how incredibly Marsalis plays on the date? It's way beyond his work on the, yes, more substantial album with the Haydn concerto. At the Village Vanguard I overheard him telling Terence Blanchard about an orchestral player in London who gave him a lesson that cleaned up his attack, and maybe the record was cut after the lesson. In any event, Wynton Marsalis has managed to transform himself from a precociously gifted interpreter into what sounds suspiciously like a great one.

Live, at the Bottom Line and two nights later at the Vanguard, he was thrilling but inconsistent. The most impressive statement, really, was his band. With Branford Marsalis, who occasionally plays better than his brother, and Kenny Kirkland, who occasionally plays better than either of them, it has three superlative soloists; while the seventeen-year-old bassist Charnett Moffett tends to overplay, he is growing into the part, and Jeff Watts is an inspiring drummer. Together they are damn near impeccable, and although it's not hard for an experienced listener to play a game of trace-the-influence, their idiom seems freshly reinvented.

Conservatism is a dead duck, but neoclassicism can be a genuine and powerful redeployment of the resources of a tradition, at times as necessary to that tradition's life— well, maybe—as any other of its possible gestures, as bracing and central to its organic life as the boldest experimentation. There are riper bands in the music, but the Marsalis quintet might turn out to be an enormous inspiration to young musicians coming up who might want to play jazz but are puzzled and finally put off by both the commercializers of fusion and an only semicomprehensible avant-garde. If so, it could be one of the best things to have happened to the music in years.

I met with Marsalis again after the Vanguard date, to touch base and chat off the record. I found him working through some new tunes for the band, teaching himself drums, eating stew for breakfast, and studying the score of Bartok's *Concerto for Orchestra*. We discussed a wide range of music—somewhere in the course of which Bartok was referred to as "a long skinny cat with a big head on top and enough dick on him for ten miles of Johnson," probably the first time the composer has been called this outside of his native Hungary—and one of the things I discovered was the range and retentiveness of Marsalis's memory. I mentioned Shostakovich and he began singing the trumpet part of the piano and trumpet concerto; I recalled a favorite Ornette Coleman solo (on "Peace") and he proceeded to sing *that*, with all its asymmetrical phrasing and bent pitches intact. Maybe this facility provides a clue to his intolerance of the deficiencies of his neighbor musicians— he sees so little reason to have any. Mozart had a similar incomprehension, and cruelty, possibly for the same reason.

Marsalis relented somewhat from his position on technique in the interview, conceding that concept was more important, though of course it was best to have both. In everything he said about music, however, there was the overwhelming urge to quantify, to substantiate every statement technically, and I saw in this the action of a powerful young mind extending its range and confirming its grasp of its subject. Brilliant young men often build their model of the universe by absolutizing their opinions and excluding everything that might contradict them. It's a way of constructing a necessary basis for creative work, and it works, but it tends to exclude the inconvenient and unquantifiable, at least until later, which is to say that the conceptual edifice, however impressive, is seldom itself absolute. Marsalis, as Dostoevsky remarked of someone who played another axe, is young, abstract, and therefore cruel. But when not talking about musicians whose work he dislikes, he's a different guy—funny, modest, sensitive, perceptive. I mentioned in passing that he was playing less and less like other people. "Yeah, I'm just beginning to pick the stuff out, you know?" he answered, in the mode that's natural to him when he's not defending himself from aliens. His gift is so large there's no telling what it'll look like when he finishes unwrapping it.

Because of a consuming lack of interest in his funk records, I went to sleep on Herbie Hancock for a number of years, but then in 1981 I caught him live with VSOP II— and was suddenly reminded what an incredibly brilliant pianist he was. Y'see, in my part of the forest the local mythology runs that when you make compromises the size of Hancock's, your music goes all to hell, and this guy onstage was a damn genius.

With McCoy Tyner, Herbie Hancock dominated mainstream jazz piano in the sixties, and if you think his influence has abated in the interim, go listen to Kenny Kirkland. Hancock's fleetness of touch and harmonic imagination are still unsurpassed in the idiom, and his accompaniments—sudden, two-handed commentaries that frame a horn soloist's statements like an instantaneous orchestration—are so unusual no one has picked up on them. And unlike most of the others who were brushed by Miles's dark wing, Hancock did not, after *Bitches Brew*, go on to some sort of hyphenated amalgam along the lines of jazz-rock, but, after the breakup of an intriguing sextet, to a personal version of straight funk. Shocking, *non?*

Once Hancock got out of straight jazz rhythms, he evinced an at least partly unexpected rhythmic genius. The asymmetrical riffs for Rhodes that turn up on Freddie Hubbard's *Straight Life* and in the even more unusual "Ostinato" on the *Mwandishi* album—Hancock's sextet seemed on the verge of conflating jazz-rock and the avant-garde in a way that even Miles never managed—fell by the wayside when the funk was engaged. But the density of interlocking rhythmic patterns that showed up on *Headhunter*'s "Sly" and even more definitively on *Thrust*'s "Actual Proof" and "Spank-a-Lee," on which the interaction between Hancock, bassist Paul Jackson, and drummer Mike Clark seems almost unplayably complex, certainly defused the charge that Hancock had sold out to a technically undemanding medium. His two-handed riffing could hardly be more polyrhythmic, and in abandoning the free-flowing jazz rhythm section that evolved inseparably alongside the language of front-line jazz improvisation over the decades, Hancock the improviser may have been less inconvenienced than anyone else making a similar move—just look at what backbeats did to Miles's sense of line. As a soloist he seems able to phrase as freely and imaginatively as he chooses, his rhythmic imagination freeing him from the brick-wall barlines that trap other pilgrims into phrases that cliché closed as regular as clockwork every two or four bars; Hancock flies past them into long, organically shaped melodic paragraphs in which the only predictable punctuation is the sound of other musicians' jaws dropping, if they bother to listen to the details in which God so famously hangs out. Hancock's harmonic invention is likewise unimpaired by his funk's relentless insistence on very basic blues.

Still, to hear him at his utter best, you may have to sit around in a recording studio, as I had the good fortune to do recently, drinking too much paper-cup coffee while waiting for the man to drift in an hour and a half late, make a couple of phone calls to the Coast, forget where he put his book of Buddhist Sutras, then sort of amble over to the piano, blink mildly at the chart, and nod at the straight-ahead jazz guys—hiya Jack, what's up Charlie, hey there Mike—who've been waiting for him awhile now. Then he comps his way through the head the wrong way once—sorry, fellas—gets it right on the second take, and then—is it my turn?—plays a little five-note phrase going into his solo that seems to interest him—his eyebrows go up, anyhow—and before you've had a moment to think about it, he's inverted the phrase, run it through a couple of increasingly chromatic variations, sent it sailing through three surprisingly related but remarkably apt keys into the next county, where it invests in property, throws a housewarming party, begets and raises a couple of kids, flies the family to a distant country for a long vacation and then comes right back home, while back in the studio maybe ten or fifteen seconds have passed, a couple of people have grabbed their heads in their hands to keep them from coming off, and Jesus has been mentioned twice. Herbie Hancock has never been an emotional powerhouse on the order, say, of McCoy Tyner, but for pure brilliant musicianship and invention, there is still no one on the instrument to match him.

Back in the real world, however, the black-tie crowd at the Grammys leapt to their feet and cheered, so did the mob I joined at the Ritz, everybody on the street digs it, it's both high-tech and low-Bronx, and even my jazz-snob friends allow that when they first heard it on the radio, "Rockit" was an obviously great novelty hit, but I dunno, dehumanization just doesn't make me wanna dance. Maybe if I were limber enough to break, I'd worry less, since breakdancing seems to me an invention of wit and maybe even genius, a demonstration, in the time-honored tradition of black music (cf. *Stompin' the Blues*), that a world that flips you upside down, hits you upside the head, throws you to the ground, and spins you like a top—you're constricted and compressed by everything the city can do to you, your feelings are insistently drained out of you, it's turning you circumscribed and robotic, your life too tight, too narrow, the angles too sharp for you to get through—that a world like this can still be dealt with and imaged into something bearable by artmagic and thrown back in its face, laughed into place by the superior powers of invention and grace inside you, that despite it all you can still find room to be human.... Hey, that ain't chopped liver. But the machine beat to which it is most often danced seems to represent pure Enemy, and the virtuoso mixes that D. St. and others come up with at the boards still sound like a portrait of a shoddy and mechanistic hell, the world reproduced but not even a little bit transformed.

I don't know what I expected from Herbie Hancock at the interview—perhaps an obligatory, pro forma defense of music he didn't really believe in—but that's not what the man is about. His disagreement with Marsalis is the one about the water in the bottle: Marsalis keeps maintaining that the water in the bottle is conditioned by the bottle, that it is tall or squat, green or blue, and Hancock keeps on saying that water is always water, music always music, essence always essence. It can be a facile point of view or a profound one. My take on recent Herbie Hancock, after listening to him talk, seeing what he's like, was that for some reason—his inextricable musicianship, or mercurial flexibility, or maybe all that *nam yoho renge kyo*—he's artistically immune to the potentially negative aspects of his choices. Marsalis couldn't function that way, ninety-nine out of a hundred musicians couldn't function that way (though hundreds have tried), but Herbie Hancock can and does. When I saw his current touring band live, I left with my head full of unwanted chugachugachugachug, the memory of an imaginative solo on "Karabali" and of Hancock playing to the audience, shadowboxing in the spotlight, stage-grinning and indulging in other antics that can get you excommunicated from the sacred body of jazz, yet he hasn't been and won't be. The new album, *Sound System*, extends the language of *Future Shock*, and probably its success, and draws some obviously fascinating parallels between boombox hiphop and its African ancestors, and most of it's still not for me. Meeting up with Herbie Hancock has been a privilege that has not altered my tastes—but it has changed my mind.

MUSICIAN: *We don't want to get you guys into an argument.*

HANCOCK: Oh, we won't, we never argue.

MARSALIS: I would never argue with Herbie.

MUSICIAN: *I'll tell what we want to start with. Is there a necessity for any young player, no matter how brilliant he is, to work his way through a tradition?*

MARSALIS: That's a hard question to answer. When we deal with anything that's European, the definitions are clear cut. But with our stuff it all comes from blues, so "it's all the same." So that'll imply that if I write an arrangement, then my arrangement is on the same level as Duke Ellington. But to me it's *not* the same. So what I'm trying to determine is this terminology. What is rock 'n' roll? What does jazz mean, or R&B? Used to be R&B was just somebody who was black, in pop music they are white. Now we know the whole development of American music is so steeped in racist tradition that it defines what we're talking about.

MUSICIAN: *Well, there's the Berklee School of Music approach, where you learn technique. And some people would say, Well, as long as it's coming from the heart, it doesn't matter about technique.*

MARSALIS: That is the biggest crock of bullshit in the history of music, that stuff about coming from the heart. If you are trying to create art, the *first thing* is to look around and find out what's meaningful to you. Art tries to make life meaningful, so automatically that implies a certain amount of emotion. Anybody can say "I have emotion." I mean, a thousand trumpet players had soul and emotion when they picked up trumpets. But they weren't all Louis Armstrong. Why?

HANCOCK: He was a better human being.

MARSALIS: Because Louis Armstrong's technique was better.

MUSICIAN: *Is that the only thing, though?*

MARSALIS: Who's to say that his soul was greater than anybody else's? How can you measure soul? Have any women left him, did he eat some chicken on Saturday night? That's a whole social viewpoint of what payin' dues is. So Duke Ellington shouldn't have been great because by definition of dues he didn't really go through as much as Louis Armstrong, so naturally his piano playing didn't have the same level of soul. Or Herbie wasn't soulful, either. Because when he was coming up, black people didn't have to eat out of frying pans on Friday nights.

MUSICIAN: *Well, one of the ways of judging soulfulness, as you say, is suffering. But it's not the only way.*

MARSALIS: I read a book [James Lincoln Collier] where a cat said that "in 1920-something we notice that Louis Armstrong's playing took on a deeper depth of emotion. Maybe that's because his mother died." What brings about soulfulness is realization. That's all. You can realize it and be the richest man in the world. You can be someone living in the heart of Harlem in the most deprived situation with no soul at all. But the social scientists . . . oh, soul. That's all they can hear, you know. Soul is part of technique. Emotion is part of technique. Music is a craft, man.

HANCOCK: External environment brings fortune or misfortune. Both of them are means to grow. And that's what soul is about: the growth or, as Wynton said, realization. To realize how to take that experience and to find the depth of that experience in your life. If you're able to do that, then everything becomes fortune.

MARSALIS: The thing that makes me most disgusted is that a lot of guys who write about the music don't understand the musicians. People have the feeling that jazz is an expression of depression. What about Louis Armstrong? To me, his thing is an expression of joy. A celebration of the human condition.

HANCOCK: Or the other concept is somebody who, out of his ignorance and stupidity, dances and slaps his sides. No concept of intelligence, focus, concentration . . . and the study, the concern. Even the self-doubt and conflict that goes into the art of playing jazz.

Look, I didn't start off playing jazz. I hated jazz when I first heard it. It sounded like noise to me. I was studying classical music, and at the same time, going to an all-black grammar school. I heard groups like the Ravens. But I really didn't have many R&B records. I was like a little nerd in school.

MARSALIS: Well, I don't know about *that*.

HANCOCK: Jazz finally made an impression on me when I saw a guy who was my age improvising. I thought that would be impossible for somebody my age, thirteen or fourteen, to be able to create some music out of his head. I was a classical player, so I had to learn jazz the way any classical player would. When it came to learning what one feels and hears as soulful nuances in the music, I actually had to learn that technically.

MARSALIS: That's interesting, because I did it the opposite way. When you put out *Headhunters* and *Thrust*, Branford and I listened to those albums, but we didn't think it was jazz. My daddy would play jazz, but I was like, Hey, man, I don't want to hear this shit. I grew up in New Orleans—Kenner, Louisiana, actually, a country town. All I ever did was play "When the Saints" and stuff. I couldn't really play, I had no technique. So when I came to high school, everybody else could play the trumpet and I was the saddest one. The first record I heard was *Giant Steps*. My daddy had all those records, but I never would listen to them. Why listen to jazz, man?

HANCOCK: None of your friends were playing it?

MARSALIS: None of the people I knew. You couldn't get no women playing jazz! Nobody had a philosophy about what life was supposed to be about. We didn't have a continuum. I never listened to Miles or Herbie. I didn't even know you played with Miles, until I was sixteen. Then when I started listening to jazz, I would only listen to a certain type. Only bebop. So I can relate to starting from a fan-type approach. But when you play music, you're going to play the way you are.

MUSICIAN: *What about your statement at the Grammys?*

MARSALIS: It was very obvious what I was saying.

HANCOCK: I have to congratulate you on that. You implied that there was good music and music that was in bad taste. Everybody wondered, "What music is he referring to?"

MARSALIS: Listen, the only statement I made was that we're trying to elevate pop music to the level of art. Not just in music. Pop culture. Pop anything. I have nothing against pop music. I listen to the radio. I'm not saying people should listen to jazz or buy jazz records, or even know the music. Just *understand* what the music is about, because the purpose and the function of pop music is totally different from jazz.

HANCOCK: A few people that have interviewed me have asked me if the statement that he made was directed against what I was doing. That never dawned on me.

MARSALIS: I wasn't even thinking about that.

MUSICIAN: *A lot of people do think that.*

MARSALIS: People think I'm trying to say jazz is greater

than pop music. I don't have to say that, that's *obvious*. But I don't even think about it that way. The two musics say totally different things. Jazz is *not* pop music, that's all. Not that it's greater. . . . I didn't mean it was obvious.

HANCOCK: That's your opinion, which is fine. Now you're making a statement of fact.

MUSICIAN: *So is classical music "greater" than jazz?*

MARSALIS: Hell no, classical music is a European idiom. America has a new cultural identity. And the ultimate achievement for any culture is the creation of an art form. Now, the basic element of our art form is the blues, because an art form makes life meaningful. Incidentally, I would like to say—and I hope you will print this—classical music is *not* white music. When Beethoven was writing music, he wasn't thinking white or black. Those terms became necessary in America when they had to take white artists and make them number one because they couldn't accept black artists. We constantly have historical redefinitions to take the artistic contributions out of the hands of people who were designated black. The root of the colloquial stuff throughout the whole world now comes out of the U.S. Negro's lifestyle.

MUSICIAN: *Is there something in some of the root forms of this music that has a certain inner strength?*

MARSALIS: People don't know what I'm doing basically, because they don't understand music. All they're doing is reacting to what they think it remotely sounds like.

We don't have to go *back* to the sixties. Beethoven didn't have to go *back* to Haydn. We never hear that. What they say is, Well, Beethoven is an extension of Haydn. Everybody has to do that—Stravinsky, Bartok. But in European music people have a cultural continuum. And our music is just, "Well, what is the next new Negro gonna think up out of the blue sky that's gonna be innovative?" Ornette Coleman sounds like Bird; he was playing rhythm changes on "The Shape of Jazz to Come." Have I ever read that by anybody reviewing those albums? No. Why? Because they don't know what rhythm changes sound like. So they're gonna write a review on what I'm doing and I'm supposed to say, "That's cool."

HANCOCK: When you first asked the question, I heard it as sensitively as he heard it. 'Cause I said to myself, He's saying Wynton is going back to play the sixties-style of music in 1984.

MUSICIAN: *We all agreed apparently at one point that jazz was more meaningful, in some sense, than pop music. Since you work in the two idioms, what do you feel is different?*

HANCOCK: Wait a minute. I *don't* agree. Let me address myself to that. When we have life, we have music. Music can be manifest in many different forms, and as long as they all have purpose, they shouldn't be pitted against each other as one being more important than the other. That's stupid. That's like apples and oranges.

MUSICIAN: *All right, you're doing both. What's the difference in the quality of the experience with each kind of music?*

HANCOCK: Let me tell you how I started getting my feet wet with pop music. When I got into high school and started getting into jazz, I didn't want to hear anything else but classical music and jazz. No R&B, nothing, until I heard James Brown's "Papa's Got a Brand New Bag." Later on, when I heard "Thank You Falettinme Be Mice Elf Agin," it just went to my core. I didn't know *what* he was doing, I mean, I heard the chorus but, how could he *think* of that. I was afraid that that was something I couldn't do. And here I am, I call myself a musician. It bothered me. Then at a certain point I decided to try my hand at funk, when I did *Headhunters*. I was not trying to make a jazz record. And it came out sounding different from anything I could think of at the time. But I still wasn't satisfied because in the back of my head I wanted to make a funk record.

I had gotten to the point where I was so directed toward always playing something different that I was ignoring the validity of playing something that was familiar. Visually I symbolize it as: There's the space from the earth up to somewhere in the sky, then I was going from the sky up to somewhere further up in the sky. And this other thing from the earth up to the sky I was kind of ignoring. And so one thing about pop music that I've discovered is that playing something that's familiar or playing the same solo you played before has no negative connotations whatsoever. What's negative is if it doesn't sound, each time, like it's the first time you played it. Now, that's really difficult for me to do. Take Wah Wah Watson, for example. He's not a solo player, he's a rhythm player. But he used to play a little solo on one tune and it would be the same solo every night. And every night he would get a bigger hand than I would. And every night it was the same notes but it sounded fresh. So my lesson was to try to learn to play something without change, and have it sound fresh and meaningful.

MARSALIS: I look at music different from Herbie. I played in a funk band. I played the same horn parts every night all through high school. We played real funk tunes like Parliament Funkadelic, authentic funk. It wasn't this junk they're trying to do now to get their music played on white radio stations. Now, to play the Haydn Trumpet Concerto is a lot different from playing "Give Up the Funk" or "Mothership Connection." I dig "Mothership Connection," but to me what pop music is trying to do is totally different. It's really geared to a whole base type of sexual thing. I listen to the radio. I know tunes that they have out now: here's people squirming on the ground, fingering themselves. It's low-level realizations of sex. Now, to me, music to stimulate you is the music that has all the root in the world in it, but is trying to elevate that, to elevate the people to a certain level rather than go down.

HANCOCK: It's not like that, Wynton. If it were, it would just stay the same. Why would the music change?

MARSALIS: Because they get new computers. You tell me, what's the newest thing out that you've heard?

HANCOCK: Okay, Prince, let's take that.

MARSALIS: What is the tune "Purple Rain"? Part of it is like a little blues. I've got the record, I listen to it all the time. The guitar solo is a rehash of some white rock.

MUSICIAN: *It's a rehash of Hendrix, too.*

MARSALIS: Well, I'm not gonna put that on his head because he can do stuff Hendrix never thought of doing, which a lot of people want to overlook just to cut him down and say he sounds like Hendrix. You can print that if you talk about him. But there's no way you can get new in that type of music because the message will always be the same.

HANCOCK: There are songs that have a lot of musical episodes. I saw Rick Springfield's video. I don't care if he's got a bad reputation. I heard some harmonic things that were really nice.

MARSALIS: You can get the newest synthesizers, but that music'll only go to a certain level. I'm not saying that's negative.

MUSICIAN: *In a sense you're describing what Herbie's doing.*

MARSALIS: He knows what he's doing, right? [*laughs*]

HANCOCK: It's *not* true because I know. You mention drum machines. There are examples of pop music today using drum machines specifically in a very automated way. Automation doesn't imply sex to me at all. It's the opposite of sex.

MARSALIS: But that's not what we're talking about.

HANCOCK: You said the music is about one thing, and it's about sex. And I'm saying it's not just about that.

MARSALIS: We don't even want to waste our time discussing that because we *know* that that's what it's about.

HANCOCK: If you name specific things, I would certainly agree with you. If you say dancing is about sex, I would agree with you, too. But I think you're using some false ammunition.

MUSICIAN: *In most of the world's traditions sex is both connected with the highest creative aspects and then can be taken to the lowest basic. . . .*

MARSALIS: That's what I'm saying. What direction you want to go with it and which level it's marketed on. When I see stuff like videos with women looking like tigers roaming through the jungle, you know, women playing with themselves, which is cool, man, but to me that's the high school point of view. The problem I have is when people look at that and start using terms like "new video art with such daring concepts."

A lot of stuff in our society is racially oriented, too. I read a quote from Herbie. He said, "I heard that people from MTV were racist oriented and I didn't want to take any chances, so when I did my video I made sure they didn't focus on me and that some of the robots' faces were white." That somebody like him would have to make a statement like that . . .

MUSICIAN: *That* is *a heavy statement.*

MARSALIS: But what he's saying is true. Maybe they wouldn't have played his video. And what pisses me off is the arrogance of people whose whole thing is just a blatant irritation of the negroidal tradition. Blatant. And even the major exponents of this type of music have said that themselves. And they'll have the arrogance and the audacity to say, Well, we just gonna play white people's videos. How am I supposed to relate to that?

MUSICIAN: *On the other hand, "Rockit" won five video awards. It partly broke open MTV; there are now more black acts on. And now kids in the heartland who have never heard black music are beginning to hear it. It's probably because of what you did.*

MARSALIS: They're still not hearing it. Black music is being broken down. It's no longer black music. This is not a discussion or argument. You get the Parliament records and the EW&F and the James Brown, the Marvin Gaye, and you listen. What I hear now is just obvious rock 'n' roll elements like Led Zeppelin. If people want to do that, fine. If they want to sell more records, great. What I'm saying is, that's reaffirmation of prejudice to me. If bending over is what's happening, I'm going to bend over.

MUSICIAN: *Is there another side? What do you think, Herbie?*

MARSALIS: Well, Wynton is not an exponent of the idea that blending of musical cultures is a good thing.

WYNTON: Because it's an *imitation* of the root. It loses roots because it's *not* a blending. It's like having sex with your daughter.

HANCOCK: Okay, let me say this because this is something that *I* know. Up until recently a black artist, even if he felt rock 'n' roll like Mick Jagger, couldn't make a rock 'n' roll record. Because the media actually has set up these compartments that the racists fit things into. You can hear *elements* of rock from black artists.

MARSALIS: You don't just hear elements. What I hear in them is blatant, to the point of cynicism.

HANCOCK: Okay, okay. I'm not disagreeing. I know that there have been black artists that have wanted to do different kinds of music than what the R&B stations would play. That to me is more important, the fact that we can't do what we want to.

MARSALIS: I'm agreeing with you, everybody should do what they want to do. But what's happening is, our vibe is being lost. I see that in movies. I see it on television. What you have now is white guys standing up imitating black guys, and black guys sitting back and looking at an imitation of us saying, "Ohhh" . . . with awe in their faces. You have black children growing up with Jehri curls trying to wear dresses, thinking about playing music that doesn't sound like our culture.

MUSICIAN: *Does Herbie "hear" what he's doing?*

MARSALIS: Herbie hears what Herbie plays. But a lot of that music Herbie is not writing. And when Herbie is playing, he's gonna make the stuff sound like Herbie playin' it.

HANCOCK: Let me explain something about "Rockit." If you're a black artist doing some forms of pop music, which "Rockit" is, you have to get on black radio and become a hit. And if you get in the top twenty in black radio, or urban contemporary they call it now [*laughter*] anyway, if it's considered crossover material, then at that point the record company will try to get the rock stations to play it. And so I said to myself, "How can I get this record exposed as quickly to the white kids as to the black kids?" So the video was a means to an end.

MUSICIAN: *Did it bother you, having to make that decision?*

HANCOCK: I didn't care about being in the video. I don't care about being on the album cover of my record. It's not important to me. Why should I have to be in my own video? [*Wynton winces*]

MUSICIAN: *But why* shouldn't *you? I mean, it's your video.*

HANCOCK: That was not an issue with me. I'm not on the cover of most of my records. What I care about is whether the cover looks good or not. I wanted the video to be good.

That's the first thing. The second thing I said: Now, how am I gonna get on there, because I want to get my record heard by these kids?

MUSICIAN: *Can't you see this strategy is a way of breaking something in?*

MARSALIS: If you cheese enough, they'll make you President.

HANCOCK: I wasn't cheesing. I was trying to get heard.

MUSICIAN: *He broke open the medium, partially.*

MARSALIS: Michael Jackson broke the medium open. Let's get that straight. What's amazing to me is that [Herbie's] thing was used by all the cats that were doing break dancing.

HANCOCK: There were three things against it. First of all, no vocals. Secondly, that kind of music wasn't even getting any airplay at that time. Third thing is my name.

MARSALIS: Right. But the only thing that I hate, the only thing that disgusts me about that is I've seen Herbie's thing on *Solid Gold* as "New Electronic" type of jazz or something. I mean, it's a *pop* tune, man. Our whole music is just going to continue to be misunderstood. You have to understand that people who hear about me, they don't listen to the music I play. If I have girlfriends, they don't listen to what I'm playing. They don't care. They only know Wynton as an image. Or Wynton, he's on the Grammys, he has a suit on. So their whole thing is media oriented. I'm not around a lot of people who listen to jazz or classical music, forget that! I did a concert and people gave me a standing ovation before I walked onto the stage. But in the middle of the first piece they were like [*nods off*] ... so that lets you know right there what's happening.

MUSICIAN: *Is this a black audience?*

MARSALIS: Black people. Yeah, this is a media thing, you understand. I'm talking to people who are in the street.

HANCOCK: I understand what you're talking about, about black artists with Jheri curls and now with the long hair. And I don't mean the Rastas, either. . . .

MARSALIS: Well, check it out. Even deeper than that, Herbie, is when I see brothers and sisters on the TV. I see black athletes, straining to conform to a type of personality that will allow them to get some more endorsements. What disturbs me is it's the best people. When somebody is good, they don't have to do that. I was so happy when Stevie's album came out. I said, Damn, finally we got a groove and not somebody just trying to cross over into some rock 'n' roll.

HANCOCK: I understand what you mean about a certain type of groove, like this is the real R&B, and so forth. But I can't agree that there's only one way we're supposed to be playing. I have faith in the strength of the black contribution to music, and that strength is always going back to the groove, anyway. After a while certain things get weeded out. And the music begins to evolve again.

MARSALIS: Now, check out what I'm saying. . . .

HANCOCK: No, 'cause you've talked a lot. . . .

MARSALIS: Okay, I'm sorry. I'm sorry, man.

HANCOCK: [*laughter*] Give me a break! I've never been on an interview with you, so I didn't know how it was. Wowww! I understand what you're saying, but I have faith that whatever's happening now is not a waste of time. It's a part of growth. It may be a transition, but transition is part of growth, too. And it doesn't bother me one bit that you hear more rock 'n' roll in black players, unless it's just not good. The idea of doing rock 'n' roll that comes out of Led Zeppelin doesn't bother me. I understand it's third-hand information that came from black people to begin with, but if a guy likes it, play it. When Tony Williams and I first left Miles, we did two different things. My orientation was from a funk thing. What Tony responded to was rock 'n' roll. That's why his sound had more of a rock influence than *Headhunters*. I can't say that's negative.

MARSALIS: I agree with what Herb has said. If somebody wants to go out with a dress on, a skirt, panties . . . that's their business. But what happens is not that one or two people do that. Everybody has to do that. It doesn't bother me that [black] comedians can be in film, I think that's great. And the films are funny. What bothers me is that *only* comedians can be in films.

I think since the sixties, with people on TV always cursing white people but not presenting any intellectual viewpoint, that any black person who tries to exhibit any kind of intellect is considered as trying not to be black. We have allowed social scientists to redefine what type of people we are. I play some European to pay respect to a great, great music which had nothing to do with racial situations. Beethoven wasn't thinking about the social conditions in America when he wrote something, he was thinking about why did he have to get off the street for the princes. So his music has the same type of freedom and struggle for abolition of the class system, as Louis Armstrong's music is a celebration of that abolition. See, Beethoven's music has that struggle in it. Louis Armstrong is the resolution of that. This gigantic cultural achievement is just going to be redefined unless I take an active part in saying what I think is correct.

HANCOCK: Now that you've voiced all—not all, but *many* of your objections—what do you do about it? How do we make it better? If all we do is complain . . .

MARSALIS: We're not complaining. We're providing people with information.

HANCOCK: Well, there's two ways to provide people with information. One way is to point your finger at them or intimidate them by pulling at their collars. But many times what that does is it makes the person feel uncomfortable, and then if he starts to get on the defensive, you've lost more ground than you've gained. So I've found from my own life that I can get more accomplished by getting a person inspired to do something. Inspiration, not intimidation.

MARSALIS: 'Cept intimidation is good, too.

HANCOCK: This is where you and I differ. I haven't said much before because I'm not like that.

MUSICIAN: *You've really defined your point of view in terms of this interview, and Herbie hasn't yet.*

MARSALIS: I was talking too much. Sorry I was being uncool.

HANCOCK: No, no, no. It was cool. It's all right. I'll come back another day when you're not here ... [*general laughter*]

MARSALIS: The problem is in the educational system. I've had conversations with people about you. Musicians have no idea who you are. They have no understanding or respect for being able to play. It's just like they think they're you or something. The first question I hear everywhere is, "How do you get over? How did you get your break with Herbie?" I said, "When I was with Herbie and them, I was just fortunate to be on the bandstand. Just to be learning from Herbie ..." No, seriously, man, I'm not saying it to kiss your ass. You know it's true.

HANCOCK: That's what I feel about him. He came in with one trumpet, nineteen years old playing with me, Ron, and Tony.

MARSALIS: I was scared.

HANCOCK: When I heard him play, then I had to call up Ron and Tony and say ...

MARSALIS: Hey, this mother is sad. [*laughs*]

HANCOCK: Look, it's gonna work. What he did was so phenomenal. You remember that tour. That tour was bad.

MARSALIS: I learned so much on that tour, man.

HANCOCK: So did I, man. You taught me a lot. You made me play. Plus you made me get some new clothes. [*laughs*]

MARSALIS: I can get publicity until I'm a hundred. That's not gonna make me be on the level with cats like Miles or Clifford, or know the stuff that you know. Even "Rockit" has elements that I can relate to. But in general you made funk cats musicians. And that has been overlooked.

MUSICIAN: *In the end, were the compromises involved in doing the video worth it?*

HANCOCK: I had a choice. And I'm proud of the choice that I made. But as a result, what happened? Between Michael Jackson's video and my video, the impact opened the thing up. Now, I'm sure Michael can take more credit for that. Anyway, if it was true that MTV was racist. . .

MARSALIS: It was true. You don't have to say "if."

HANCOCK: I have never claimed that to be true.

MARSALIS: I'll say it.

HANCOCK: I've only claimed that this is what I observe. But now you see plenty of videos with black artists. It doesn't even look like there's any difference anymore. Even though I wasn't even looking for that as a solution, if this additional thing was accomplished, I feel really good about that. And I feel good about getting five awards on MTV. They were trying to copy something before. Now they realize they have something that's more powerful than what they were trying to copy.

MARSALIS: The sound of Michael Jackson's music, the sound of Prince's music, the sound of "Rockit"—that sound is *not* black. People are consciously trying to be crossovers. I've read interviews where people say, "We take this type of music and we try to get this type of sound to appeal to this type of market to sell these many records."

MUSICIAN: *Do you think Michael did that?*

MARSALIS: Of course he did. But the thing that separates

Michael Jackson from all other pop artists is the level of sincerity in his music.

MUSICIAN: *You're saying he's got sincerity, and yet at the same time he contoured his sound?*

MARSALIS: He's a special person. He's not contrived. What I don't understand is why he did that cut with Mick Jagger.

HANCOCK: I'll tell ya, I just did a record with Mick Jagger and, man, Mick Jagger's *bad*.

MARSALIS: Yeah, well . . .

HANCOCK: I didn't know that. And you don't know that, either.

MARSALIS: I'm not doubting that he's bad. . . .

HANCOCK: Wynton, you *don't* know that.

MARSALIS: I'm not doubting that he's bad, Herbie. Check it out. But a lot of pop music is geared toward children. It's not something that I can really have a serious discussion about.

HANCOCK: You're right. It's geared toward teens and the preteens. So what it's doing is stimulating my own youth and allowing me to express my own youth. Because it's not like I'm doing my daughter's music. This is *my* music. And we both happen to like it because we both feel that youthful element. People tell me I look younger now than I did five years ago. And I do . . . except in the morning. [*laughs*] I would venture to say that a lot of it has to do with the music I'm playing now. Electric music, you know. I'm finding a door that hasn't been opened. That's exciting me, and I'm given the opportunity to use some elements from the "farthest out" jazz stuff in this music, and have it be unique.

MUSICIAN: *How do you get human feeling in automated, computerized music like that?*

HANCOCK: First we create the music. Afterwards I sit back and listen, and sometimes I discover things that I wasn't really thinking about when I was doing them. I hear the elements that have warmth. Sometimes it's a particular synthesizer sound. But it could be how it's played.

MARSALIS: I'm coming off negative and that's not what I'm intending. . . . The purpose of pop music is to sell records that appeal to people on a level that they want to accept it on. If you put out a record and it doesn't sell, then your next response is, Why didn't the record sell? Let's try to do this or that to make the record sell.

MUSICIAN: *That's terribly condescending toward pop. . . .*

HANCOCK: Why are we asking him about pop music? What does *he* know about pop music?

MARSALIS: I know a lot about pop music.

HANCOCK: No, you don't.

MARSALIS: I played in pop. . . .

HANCOCK: Wynton, you don't. You *think* you know.

MARSALIS: I don't want to mess with you.

HANCOCK: The very statement that you just made makes it obvious that you don't know.

MARSALIS: That's cool. I'm not going to get into it. I've had conversations with you, where you told me, "Man we're trying to get this kind of market." It's not like I don't know pop musicians. It's not like I don't listen to music.

HANCOCK: Then there's some things you misunderstand about it. Because I *never* use the word *sell*.

MARSALIS: I don't know. Remember what you told me before? "Yeah, man, my record just went gold, man. I need to get me some more records like that." We had long conversations about that. We shouldn't be arguing about this in the press, man. We have to be cool. We've talked about this already.

HANCOCK: Do you think I'd object if my records sold millions?

MARSALIS: Don't say you don't think about that.

HANCOCK: Of course I would.

MARSALIS: Because you do. You *do* think about that.

MUSICIAN: *To think about it and have it as your aim are two different things.*

HANCOCK: Thank you.

MARSALIS: I'm getting tired now. You said the opposite of what I wanted to hear.

HANCOCK: Look, I'd like to have a Rolls-Royce, too. But I'm not purposefully trying to set myself up to get a Rolls-Royce.

MARSALIS: Pop music is something that you don't really have to know too much to know about.

HANCOCK: [*long silence*] . . . Okay, next!

MUSICIAN: *When you play pop music, do you feel as musically fulfilled as when you're playing jazz?*

MARSALIS: Don't lie, Herbie.

HANCOCK: Okay. I only feel musically fulfilled when I can do both. If I don't play any jazz this year or half of next year, I'm gonna still be doing fine. But at a certain point I'm gonna want to play some. Now, what I wanted to say was when I did "Rockit," when I did *Light Me Up* . . . I'm not sitting down and saying, "What can I put in this music to make it sell?" That's what I *don't* do. When I'm sitting and actually making the music, I know my frame of mind. And you can't tell me . . .

MARSALIS: I can't tell you anything. . . .

HANCOCK: No, I'm being honest. Let's say you want to do cartoons, or make a comic book, and you're Gauguin. If Gauguin were to do a comic book, I would respect him if he had the same kind of attitude of trying to make something happen with the cartoon, and learn from dealing with a medium that's more popular than the one he's accustomed to.

MUSICIAN: *What he's also saying is there's this evolutionary sweep that takes all these things in its stride. . . .*

HANCOCK: I'm not looking at these things that you're objecting to as the end. I look at them more as an interim.

MARSALIS: It's just ignorance being celebrated to the highest level. If somebody wants to say anything that has any kernel of intellect, immediately the word *elitist* is brought out and brandished across the page to whip them back down into ignorance. Especially black artists and athletes. We are constantly called upon to have nothing to say. I'm just trying to stimulate ... some kind of intellectual realization. I'm just trying to raise questions about why we as musicians have to constantly take into account some bullshit to produce what we want to produce as music, what Herbie is saying about evolution. Frankly, I never thought about it that way. But he brought out something interesting. All I can say is, I hope he's right.

CHET BAKER

BY JEROME REECE

■

Another night, another club:

For Chet Baker it is the same story as yesterday, as tomorrow, as twenty-five years ago. A set, a break, another set, sweat. Science fiction lighting adds to the haziness of time and period; everywhere, in the inevitable mirrors and even in the floor, one can contemplate one's image. Without a microphone the sounds flowing from his trumpet would be but a murmur barely more perceptible than his voice—a voice so much softer than the profoundly marked face that only opens enough to let it filter out.

It is hard to believe that he was once called the James Dean of jazz. Chet Baker's face, which bears an eerie resemblance to Antonin Artaud's in the last part of his life, is now but a fascinating mask sculpted by the trials of life and creation.

Without his glasses he seems even farther away, lost in an opaque fog. Chet sees little, but enough to instinctively piece together the listening forms and shadows. Enough in any case to guess, night after night, the other side of the spectacle: the bartender shaking a cocktail, the waitress moving back and forth in front of the stage, the noisy silhouettes leaning on tables.

Even when he's not playing, Chet grips his trumpet like a weapon; he continually licks the embouchure and his elastic face invents new wrinkles. And if he gets up to sing, his hand keeps looking for imaginary pistons on the microphone. Mysteriously, time and tobacco have only polished his voice, with its imperceptible falsetto that plays every register of feeling. Virtuoso instrumentalist and tightrope singer, Chet has arrived at an extraordinary osmosis of two forms of musical expression, comparable to the great blues singers/harmonical players.

Chet Baker has been a star in Europe for almost thirty years. He has spent the major portion of his career there, beginning with his first, triumphant visit to Paris in 1955. He'd grown up in California; his father had played banjo and guitar in various swing bands. A few cursory lessons in junior high school comprised the whole of Chet's formal musical training; later, as a member of an army band, he learned to sight-read by picking up marches by ear and then transposing what he'd heard to the printed sheets before him. Discharged in 1948, he flunked his theory classes at El Camino College in L.A., then reenlisted to join the Presidio army-band station in San Francisco, and not coincidentally, join the nightly jam sessions at Bop City with the likes of Dexter Gordon, Paul Desmond, and Hampton Hawes. By 1952 he was playing West Coast dates with Charlie Parker. The following year he joined the Gerry Mulligan quartet, where the chemistry between Mulligan's probing baritone and Baker's light, lilting trumpet thrust both toward international prominence. By 1953, the year he began recording under his own name, Baker had already won the *Down Beat* poll as the best trumpet player in jazz. He was twenty-four years old.

With its lyrical West Coast sound, the Mulligan-Baker quartet dominated jazz in the early and mid-fifties. Baker's fresh, openly romantic style hasn't really changed much over the years, but his subsequent experiences have given his sound an edge that's intensely melancholic and bittersweet. His problems began almost before he had a chance to savor success—first a gum disease that threatened to destroy his health and career, then a lengthy bout with heroin that effectively accomplished the same end. Arrests and prison stretches in Europe commenced with a drug bust in Italy in 1959; in 1968, in San Francisco, Baker suffered a mugging that ultimately resulted in the loss of his teeth. He stopped playing for two years, began a slow recovery from his addiction through methadone, and culminated his comeback with a reunion concert with Mulligan and several club dates around New York City in 1974–75. Then he migrated back to Europe. But, as with Miles Davis, whose muted blue tone Baker's own has long resembled, fate's scars have only deepened the inexpressible beauty of his art. If, as it has been said, Miles sounds like a man walking on eggshells, Chet sounds like Goethe's Werther singing to himself on the edge of a precipice. Along with a handful of others, he remains one of the last great jazz musicians in an ever-shrinking world where few recall what that "jazz" ever meant—though perhaps (ironically) Baker's exquisite solo on Elvis Costello's "Shipbuilding" might broaden the chance of his discovery by another generation of fans.

It's four A.M. The magical intimacy inside the club has dissipated with the last encore. Covered with sweat, Chet timidly holds his trumpet case like a junior executive with a briefcase. I ask him, stupidly enough, how he can stand all these nights in claustrophobic, smokey basements. He smiles slightly: "Lots of practice." For years he has refused interviews—this time, and who knows why—he says yes.

Several days later we meet at the country home of one of his musicians. Chet sits up on his bed, then for hours lies there with his eyes closed, sucking on candy after candy and cigarette after cigarette. At the end he gets up and, with a malicious smile, shows me his trumpet, telling me it's a student model. The music is in him, no matter what object. As I ready to leave he puts a Walkman over my ears. He smiles, always a rare moment, and gives me the cassette as a good-bye present.

MUSICIAN: *You call yourself a loner. Have you ever tried to settle down?*

BAKER: A couple times. Once in 1974 in upstate New York, with my wife and children. But when the people in the neighborhood found out who I was—through something about me on the local TV station—they started bothering my children, breaking my windows. Calling me "drug addict" in the street. The civilized world we live in is a lot of crap. I tried again a little later on Long Island and that didn't work either. People think I'm some kind of scum, so I just gave up the whole idea. Yeah, we moved out. My kids are grown up now. I don't have to worry about them. None of them are musicians.

MUSICIAN: *Are you happy about that?*

BAKER: Yeah, I'm happy about that. Yes I am. The odds against a talented musician being successful are so great. . . .

MUSICIAN: *And how do you feel about your music now?*

BAKER: It's just my way of improvising and of bouncing off what the other musicians are playing. I respond very much to what is going on around me, since I play a hundred percent by ear. The conditions I grew up in don't exist anymore. I think I'm part of a dying breed. Yeah, it's kind of sad in a way, but that's progress, I guess.

MUSICIAN: *The end of a certain jazz.*

BAKER: A certain kind of jazz, a very personal kind of jazz. There aren't too many groups anymore like the trio I have, especially without drums. It makes it more like a chamber trio. I'd prefer to play completely acoustic. The louder the music is, it seems the more people talk. But in many places people do listen. In some clubs in Paris you can hear a pin drop.

MUSICIAN: *Speaking of progress, don't you think conditions are better now than for, say, Charlie Parker in the 1940s?*

BAKER: I think Charlie Parker had a very happy life. He had tremendous success, was loved and adored by so many people. He was the king, the same as the king of a country. Playing with Bird was the very greatest experience I ever had. But I was too young and too stupid to get as much out of it as I should have. I did get to spend a lot of time with Bird—on the stand and off. I would drive him around, go to the beach . . . we got to be good friends. He certainly told me to stay away from drugs, and he kept certain people away from me who would have tried to give me things. I was twenty-two at the time, and I didn't start taking drugs until I was twenty-seven. Although people seem to think that I started much earlier.

MUSICIAN: *It's hard to believe you. You were playing with users like Gerry Mulligan, Dick Twardzick, Art Pepper . . .*

135

BAKER: I know, but I was totally clean. As clean as a whistle. Dick's overdose [while on tour with Baker in 1955] totally destroyed me. Destroyed me. Dick's parents felt it was my fault, even though I was completely unaware of this situation.

MUSICIAN: *So why did you start at twenty-seven?*

BAKER: Because I had to find out about it. I'd been fascinated for a long time, but I'd managed to fight it off. Then I started, in the States. I had gotten married a second time, which was a great mistake. She was a wonderful person, but . . .

MUSICIAN: *And you were less popular than you had been in the early fifties. . . .*

BAKER: That could have been a reason, too . . . could have been. It's not because of the "jazz world." It depends on the person. Some musicians were afraid to try drugs because they had a certain success and didn't want to jeopardize it. I'm not like that. I've been up and down so many times. . . . I have no property, no bank account, no money, and I probably will die broke—which is fine because that's the way I came into the world. I don't get any money from all those records I made. Just the advance. I've been cheated out of my record royalties by almost every company. I have no idea how many records I sell.

MUSICIAN: *So, for you, do drugs have anything to do with the way a musician plays?*

BAKER: No, I could have played just as well without it. I don't think it hurt it, but I don't think it did it any good. It gets in the way when you're strung out and have to play sick on the stand. I don't need drugs for inspiration. The music comes from inside, and is pushed out by outside influences from the musicians I'm playing with. I love to play, and I think it's the only reason I was put here on this earth.

MUSICIAN: *You say that in a religious sense.*

BAKER: Yes. But I don't believe there is a God. It's a beautiful story, but ... I'was put here through thousands of years of people having children and it finally got to me. And my father was a good musician, he had a good ear, good time.

MUSICIAN: *So you really feel you were put here to be a jazz musician?*

BAKER: Yeah, I really do. If I'd played another kind of music, I would have been more successful and wouldn't be playing anymore. I'd be retired by now.

MUSICIAN: *And it all started when your father gave you a trumpet, at thirteen.*

BAKER: Well, my father wanted me to play trombone, since he liked Jack Teagarden very much. But I was too small physically to be able to play it. I was rather small for my age. So my father got me a trumpet.

MUSICIAN: *In California?*

BAKER: Yeah, we'd moved from Oklahoma. I'd been playing about six months when a rock hit me in the left front tooth, chipping it. And I played that way for about twenty-five years. That, of course, made me invent my own technique of playing the trumpet, having that tooth missing.

MUSICIAN: *It's assumed—erroneously, I think—that you were influenced by Miles Davis. You were both growing up at the same time, and none of the trumpet players were playing in the style you both developed. It was Roy Eldridge and then Dizzy Gillespie.*

BAKER: It's a style that I evolved myself. Yes. Yes.

MUSICIAN: *But who were you listening to in your youth?*

BAKER: I listened to a lot of saxophone players. Quite a bit of Lester Young. Wardell Gray and Dexter Gordon. Wardell and Dexter lived in California. The trumpet players I knew were very young, like myself. Jack Sheldon, Pete and Conte Candoli. Also Art Farmer. We were influencing each other, and influenced by the saxophone players in L.A. at the time: Art Pepper, Lennie Niehaus, Joe Maini, Bill Perkins, Richie Kamuca.

MUSICIAN: *Were you listening to singers?*

BAKER: Not really. I admired Frank Sinatra and Mel Tormé, Tony Bennett, and Steve Lawrence also.

MUSICIAN: *You made your first record as a singer in 1954 for World Pacific* [Chet Baker Sings]. *Had you been singing since childhood?*

BAKER: Yes. My mother made me enter talent contests as a singer in the L.A. area. I'd compete against girl accordion players, tap dancers, etc. I never won, but I came in second once. I'd sing songs like "That Old Black Magic" and "I Had the Craziest Dream." It was a lot of fun, and good experience. In 1954 Dick Bock, the owner of World Pacific, suggested that I make a record as a singer. He'd heard me sing a few times in clubs—I'd sing maybe a tune a set. I never sang when I was with Gerry Mulligan. Only on our recording of "My Funny Valentine," in the studio in 1953. People really loved it or they hated it.

MUSICIAN: *Another question about your childhood. Is it true that you smoked marijuana with your parents when you were growing up?*

BAKER: No. And I don't know how that story got invented and circulated. My father would smoke with other musicians a few times a week at the house, but I was very young at the time. I never smoked with my family. What a ridiculous story—my mother was very strict and she was against all that.

MUSICIAN: *And now since we've come to that period in your life, the early Fifties, the inevitable question about Gerry Mulligan . . .*

BAKER: Playing again with Gerry is out of the question. He just doesn't want to have anything to do with me. He's so pissed off. Because I've been able to make it on my own, without him. He can't hack that. I was supposed to be his trumpet player for life, I guess. And at ridiculous wages. Which is why I left him in the first place. He wouldn't give me a raise, and I'd just been voted the best trumpet player in the world.

MUSICIAN: *You did make that CTI live reunion album together in 1974. . . .*

BAKER: We did that just for old times' sake. You can imagine how many people come up to him and ask him when he and I will play together again. It just drives him out of his mind. It's so stupid, because even if we only got together for only one year, for a world tour, it could be fantastic economically. But he won't do it.

MUSICIAN: *In 1965 you made that nice* Plays Billie Holiday *album. Did you listen to a lot of Billie Holiday, especially her last years?*

BAKER: I never listened to anyone a lot.

MUSICIAN: *That fascinated me in Art Pepper's book* [Straight Life], *and in Charles Mingus's book, too* [Beneath the Underdog]; *they hardly ever talk about music or other musicians.*

BAKER: I found Art Pepper's book kind of disgusting. All that shit about how good-looking he was, his peeping into bathroom windows . . . masturbating. Art was really a loner, but not in the same way I am. It was very difficult to get to know him. People like Pepper and Mingus were a little too preoccupied with their genitals. I realized at a very tender age that there just isn't time or opportunity enough to screw every beautiful woman in the world. It's better to just be cool—if that is possible—and to be selective and wait for the opportunity. I can't really comment on Art because I never really knew him, never got high with him, not even once. I was always rather disappointed with Art's playing when we recorded in the 1950s. He wasn't completing any ideas—things were broken up into fragments. There were no long lines. But I never got to hear him live. I heard that in the 1970s his playing was twice as good as it had ever been.

MUSICIAN: *What did you do between 1969 and 1973 when you quit playing?*

BAKER: I had my other front tooth knocked out in 1969. My teeth were in bad shape anyway from all the drugs; I had so much pain that I decided to have them all pulled out. I got a denture, and when I tried to play again I couldn't even get a sound out of the trumpet. So I quit playing. I worked in a gas station sixteen hours a day for almost two years. Then I tried again, looking for a new embouchure. It took me two years. By the summer of 1973 I felt I was ready to try to go back to work. So I was driving to New York and stopped in a club in Denver to hear Dizzy Gillespie. I told him what I was doing and he called a club in New York from his hotel and I was hired for a two-week gig in New York. And that's how I started playing again. Then I went to Europe, and found the audiences very receptive. And now I find myself working in Europe seventy-five percent of the time.

MUSICIAN: *Why do you spend so much time in Europe?*

BAKER: It's very difficult to work regularly in the States. In New York if you work in a club you can't play in a club in New York before or after for a least a month—it's in the contract. So you have to travel. It's a lot easier to travel in Europe. And the level of comprehension is much higher than in the States. The average listener in the States has the mentality of a twelve-year-old.

MUSICIAN: *You've made a lot of records over the years. Are you happy with them, or were a lot of them for the money?*

BAKER: I always need the money. I'm fairly happy with the results. I would say seventy percent of the records are worthwhile musically. Of the recent ones, *Broken Wing*

[Inner City] is very nice. *Two a Day* [Steeplechase] is nice. I've recorded a lot recently, mostly live club dates. In 1982 I did one in New York, which I like a lot, I wish it would come out, but the producer—a guy in the garment industry—is having problems. There's Kenny Barron, James Newton, Charlie Haden, Howard Johnson, and Ben Riley.

MUSICIAN: *You recently recorded with Elvis Costello ("Shipbuilding," on* Punch the Clock *for Columbia). How'd that come about?*

BAKER: I'd never heard of him. I was working in London and he contacted me. He is a very nice man. He is the only person not from the jazz world who has contacted me so far for a record date.

MUSICIAN: *He added some nice little electronic touches to your solo. Does working more with electronics interest you?*

BAKER: Not really. It would be fun to try to do it. But most jazz record companies don't seem to be interested in that. They want me to keep it ... simple. For my public.

MUSICIAN: *You've always loved Miles. What do you think of his electronic playing, as of 1969?*

BAKER: I think Miles enjoys doing things that upset people. I prefer his playing of twenty years ago, but I find what he's doing now just as valid.

MUSICIAN: *Do you hear many young trumpet players you like? Musicians influenced by you?*

BAKER: Yes, I think my style of trumpet playing is coming back a little. After all, how fast can you play? It's much more musical and certainly more—in my way of thinking anyway—difficult to play in a style where you play less notes and leave more open spaces and choose the notes you play very carefully. Playing a beautiful ballad is very difficult.

MUSICIAN: *More difficult than playing a fast bebop tune?*

BAKER: Well, of course, some of the bop tunes are very complicated, and if you try to play them at bright tempos, you triple the difficulty, and you get to the point where it's so difficult that it's no fun anymore—just a lot of hard work. And most people listening can't follow you anyway.

MUSICIAN: *Your music is often so pretty that people may not realize just how complex it really is.*

BAKER: I've been thinking about that a lot. It does look like it's a little too easy. I'm just sitting in a chair with my legs crossed. That's part of the problem. I'll have to make it look a lot more difficult somehow. But, you know, I've been playing for forty years. Why does it have to look so difficult? It's difficult to do, anyway. But this, of course, is a problem because people can't relate to that; if it doesn't look hard, then it must be easy to do. And if it's easy, then it can't be much.

MUSICIAN: *There's a definite singing quality to your trumpet playing. Do you hear the notes that way in your head?*

BAKER: Oh yeah. All the time. Anything I play on the horn I can sing. I think of every note I play. Once in a while I'll play something that's rather cliché-ish, because there are only a certain number of ways to get through a chord progression of a standard unless you really want to take it out.

MUSICIAN: *How do you keep your lip in such good shape?*

BAKER: Oh, the main thing is to play every night. I can play about two to three hours a night before I get tired. I don't practice at all, so even if there's one night in the week I don't play, the next night I notice it in my playing at first. I have to play every night.

MUSICIAN: *You play so much, aren't you sick of playing?*

BAKER: Right now I enjoy playing. It means a lot that I have musicians with me that I have good vibrations with. It makes me feel like giving everything I have. It's not always that way—sometimes I find myself in cities with musicians that I don't like and I really don't want to play.

MUSICIANS: *When are you going to stop?*

BAKER: Within five years. And if I ever teach I'd like to get kids not to depend so much on the music on the paper. Look at Berklee, that's a good example of the problem. There are shortcuts you can show kids that could give them a different insight into music that would save them a lot of time. To make them understand that improvising is a complete separate art in itself, outside the mechanics of the knowledge of chords, etc.

MUSICIAN: *You don't compose much. Your piece, "Blue Gilles," on the* Broken Wing *album is beautiful.*

BAKER: It's hard for me to compose. By the time I notate it, I've already thought of five other ways it could be. By the end I'm frustrated with the way it sounds—it could always be better. The way it could have been. Since I play by ear I do it all in my head, but someday I hope to have a place and piano. Then maybe it would be easier to get things done. I'd like to write a few things before I give up for good.

MUSICIAN: *Could we talk a bit about other trumpet players? Don Cherry, for instance.*

BAKER: I knew him from way back at jam sessions in California in the mid-fifties. I liked Don's playing with Ornette later, but it's not my taste at all.

MUSICIAN: *Clifford Brown?*

BAKER: [*a big smile*] Now, that was a sweet man. There was no race problem with him at all. I had the chance to hear him live. Trumpet playing would be different today if he were still alive. He was another man who was put here to play trumpet.

MUSICIAN: *Booker Little?*

BAKER: [*another big smile*] Oh yeah! I liked him very much. And Blue Mitchell and Kenny Dorham.

MUSICIAN: *You used to run around with Lee Morgan.*

BAKER: I didn't like him as a person, so it was hard for

me to care about his playing. Morgan and I used to go up to Harlem together to cop and to get high, and if you turned your back for a second, he'd shoot up all the stuff. If I don't like someone, I won't be able to like his music.

MUSICIAN: *Yeah, but even Charlie Parker had a rough reputation. . . .*

BAKER: He never did anything bad to me. Though I do know that he would borrow instruments from people and then pawn them. It's a terrible thing to do. But I don't think that Bird would ever have done anything like that to me. I used to go up to Harlem a lot. At one point I knew everybody. I could go alone anytime at night and walk down the street and everybody would say, "Hey" . . . you know. But not now, all those people are gone.

MUSICIAN: *So, do you think heroin is as present in jazz now as it was before?*

BAKER: No, I think it's pretty much a part of the past. One reason is that it becomes so expensive so quickly. And if you're depending on jazz to make money—hah—you can't earn enough money. And if you like cocaine to make speedballs, then you need to earn twice that to mix the two together. And you need to find all that money every day. Drugs were much cheaper in the fifties, and the quality was much better. You could buy really good heroin for three dollars. It's so expensive now, no one can afford it. Which is good, I guess.

MUSICIAN: *Speaking of drugs, you smoke way too much tobacco. You don't do anything for your voice and yet it sounds great. Every time I hear you sing your voice is different.*

BAKER: I do smoke too much, but I don't know why my voice changes the way it does. I just have to learn each night how to get around my voice. I have noticed in the past few weeks that the people who come to hear me react especially well to the numbers in the set when I sing.

MUSICIAN: *Art Pepper told me a year before his death that every time he played he was playing as if it were the last time.*

BAKER: Yeah, I play every set as though it could be my last set, too. It's been like that for several years now. Because I don't have a lot of time left and I want to show the musicians playing with me—more than anybody else—that I'm giving it all I have. I don't want anyone holding back.

BAKER'S INGREDIENTS

For a while now I've been playing a Beuscher student model. My trumpet—a Conn Constellation model—was stolen in New York and someone gave me this Buescher. It's similar to a Bach trumpet. I've been playing Conn for years. They're beautiful horns, but they're so expensive. The Conn is a very difficult instrument to play. It's very heavy to hold, and the upper register is hard to play, but the tone in the middle and lower registers is very beautiful, very dark. I played a Martin Committee for years, until the man who was responsible for the workmanship of Martin died. The company changed, and I lost interest. I used to go to the Martin factory quite often and I'd spend a whole day walking around and trying the horns until I found one that I liked.

—May 1984

MILES DAVIS

IS A LIVING LEGEND

AND YOU'RE NOT

BY MARK ROWLAND

■

The first winter storm of the season has already knocked out parts of the Pacific Coast Highway south of Los Angeles, while north, on the road to Malibu, road crews try to shove the sandy cliffs back from their inexorable march to the sea. Past where tight clusters of fragile houses hug the gold coast, then unknot and begin to scatter; past the beaches with their musical names—Paradise, Zuma, Cabrillo—and the tideline that reigns those glassy waters like the necklace of a giant pendant, now sparkling in the sun; on to where the road rises and falls in relative desolation, then rises high enough again to frame a luxurious vista above the blue Pacific: Miles Davis lives here.

The house is a modern gray box, inscrutable to outsiders. There is African art and sculpture on the walls and nestled in alcoves. Also some of Davis's own paintings, a black Yamaha baby grand, a Christmas tree with open packages scattered around, and overstuffed wicker furniture surrounding the fireplace and home-entertainment system, a stylish mix of culture and creature comfort. Miles is outfitted in similar fashion, wearing a softly patterned African shirt and gold bracelet, parachute pants, shades and slippers. A gracious host, he leads the way to the back terrace, where a steeply sloped landscape reaches down to a broad, white beach. Standing on a bench, he spreads his arms and surveys the realm. He looks like a little king, and when he speaks that familiar rasp seems to echo in the noise from the surf breaking below.

"I was out here once before, in 1946, when Bird got sick," he remembers. "I came out here with Benny Carter's band, just to see how he was. They had put him in [the mental health facility at] Camarillo. I went out to see him. He was sedated, but he knew I was there. They had him behind a wire fence, and it was real dark. I stayed there and talked to him, and he didn't say nothin'. That shit fucked me up."

He shakes his head at the memory. "We never did talk much. But I had a deep feeling for Bird. And when you give an artist like that shock treatment—and that's what they did—you know, your fingers don't move anymore. I thought, 'Goddamn!' I just left Benny Carter's band after that.

"I stayed with Lucky Thompson, for about a year; Lucky had stayed with me in New York. Lucky liked to box, you know; he was a second in the ring. I just did it for the exercise. If I want to learn something, I get the best to teach me. So I got Bobby McClellan. He knows all the stuff Joe Louis was doing, like that swirling with your ass?" Miles demonstrates with a sharp swivel. "That was hard, took me three months to get that.

"I was a good friend of Ray Robinson. Watching him train as diligently as he did, it made me break my heroin habit. The man was in shape ten months out of the year. Goddamn! And then the beauty, how he did things. I never saw anybody like that."

Though Miles no longer partakes in the sweet science ("You can't get too much into it if you work with your hands"), at sixty he's in fighting trim and playing up a storm. It's an amazing transformation for a man who, at the turn of this decade, was a virtual recluse who could barely walk and hadn't picked up a trumpet in years.

"I just swim all the time now, an hour a day, for about the last year," he reveals. "And when I got a new hip, my doctor said, 'I don't know what you're doing, but you keep on doing it.'

"When they went into my hip," he goes on, "they were supposed to stay four hours, and they stayed about ten, 'cause they found out there was nothing there. Can you imagine that? It was like being dead for ten hours. I woke up, and it was dark. Cicely [Tyson, Davis's wife] was there saying, 'You're doing fine, Miles. . . .' You know, when you wake up in the recovery room, the pain is something else. But I can walk straight now.

"I think dying should be about the same, right? Except that you'd drift into it, and I think you'd know you weren't going to wake up. So you could direct it. Have a jury trial to decide whether you're going to heaven or hell. Put your assets and your faults, your assets and your faults . . ." His voice drifts away for a moment, as if he's already going over some personal calculations. Then he smiles. "But I think they'll say, 'Well, he's the only one who can play like that; we better let him in.' "

Far down by the water, a young woman has stopped in her tracks, and now gazes in startled recognition at one of Malibu's less likely natural resources. Miles waves and calls out playfully, "Hello dear . . . hi . . ." But the breeze quickly carries off his fragile croak. When he turns back, his mood seems more philosophical. "When the time comes, I don't think I'll really die," he says. "The spirit will still be there. I am gonna wear this body out, though, 'cause I'm wearing it out now."

MY LUNCH WITH MILES

Visitors are dropping by. Miles's sister Dorothy arrives with a friend and settles on the back deck. Miles's manager comes by with an associate; they lounge in the living room. A personal assistant fixes up a tasty tuna salad ("my recipe," Miles notes proudly), and the trumpeter sides over toward the kitchen. Miles is a cook of some renown, but a light eater.

He's been performing with his nine-piece ensemble the last three evenings at Los Angeles's Universal Amphitheater, opening for Al Jarreau. Compared to recent atmospheric studio efforts like *Tutu*, the ferocity and invention of these concerts is surprising. By now, of course, just Miles showing up qualifies as an "historical event," as an Amphitheater emcee put it, but he wasn't there to be worshiped as a relic. His solos were by turns exciting and exquisite, cushioned by subtly layered rhythmic arrangements. And the electronic juggernaut he's assembled behind him— including three banks of keyboards, a funky bass pulse, two Trane-minded saxophonists, and a young guitarist seemingly weaned on "Purple Rain"—dug deep, dense, danceable grooves that Cameo fans would scream for.

Even Al Jarreau's crowd—not exactly on the cutting edge of rock, funk, *or* jazz—responded with generous ovations.

But Miles was pissed. He wanted to play longer.

"Listen, any time they tell you to play an hour," he says with disgust, "that's not like a concert to me, that's like a duty. My band is used to playing two, two and a half hours. We just played twenty-two concerts all over Europe, we had eight, ten, sixteen thousand people, and they were on everything we played; they knew all about *Tutu*. When we played in Detroit, everybody got up and danced. But here, I don't know if they were here to see me or Al Jarreau. I could have stayed home. I could have been in the audience listening to Al Jarreau. I don't care if they give me a hundred thousand dollars a minute; I'm never going to do anything like that again, ever."

He gestures toward his manager in the next room, who's happily oblivious to the conversation, and adds confidentially, "That's the reason I'm getting ready to knock him out. I hate for people to tell me that I have to play because 'an audience will watch you that would never watch you if you were by yourself.' I don't think like that." He jerks his head in the direction of his manager again. "That, for me, is like an invitation for me to murder him."

Miles is justly proud of his current lineup, several of whom (bassist Daryl Jones, keyboardist and nephew Robert Irving, and tenor saxophonist Bob Berg) have been with him for years; guitarist Dwayne "Blackbyrd" McKnight and saxophonist Gary Thomas were making their first public appearance with Miles at the Amphitheater. Although mellowed in other ways, Miles remains a restless and demanding leader whose critiques range from candid to caustic.

"I like the way Blackbyrd plays guitar," he says, "and when he finally hears the sound that's in his head, he's going to be something else. Gary too, and Bob's playing his ass off. But Bob's feeling a little funny, now that Gary's there. *Only* because my road manager, who talks too fuckin' much, says to him, 'Hey, Miles's got a new sax player.' So then Bob says to me, 'The guy's playin' my shit.' I said, '*Look*, Bob, I had Coltrane and Cannonball together! What the fuck are you talkin' about?' I mean, how can you think like that? But you know, he's got a little chesty since he put a microphone in his tenor. I told him, 'Bob, you play too fuckin' loud, you play too *long. . . .*'

"I tell you," Miles sighs, "a man's ego is something else. Especially a white man. I mean, it's not his band! But I can tell the difference in his playing since Gary's here," he concludes with some satisfaction. "And you don't want a critic to say, 'He played a chorus and he liked it so well he played it three times.' You don't want to hear that. Do you?"

Before anyone can interject the opinion that Bob Berg may also be the best tenor saxophonist Miles has had since Wayne Shorter, he goes on to explain the deeper problem: how long solos can crack the band's rhythmic foundation. "Solo players have a bad habit of starting out like they're gonna do everything themselves," Miles observes, "but it's not them—it's what we do behind them, and we can only do it for a certain length of time. I try to tell them"—Miles grins sweetly—"in a *nice* way. They say, 'You make me feel paranoid.' I say, "Well, you feel paranoid, or I feel sick.' But musicians are like that. Wayne used to get drunk and then try to play himself sober. And Tony [Williams] would just go, *whap!* And he'd stop.

"The reason I play is to hear the band that I have play," he continues evenly. "But if they play too loud I tell them to get down, and if they don't, I wait till they do. It doesn't bother me to wait, it only bothers me if they don't do it, or if it gets unbalanced. But I know they can do it, because

I've heard 'em. I wouldn't tell them to get down if I hadn't heard them do it before.

"And if they don't get down, and I have to come up," he says soberly, "that takes away the trumpet sound, and then I want to kill myself. Because I've practiced on my tone for almost . . . fifty years, and if I can't hear my tone, I can't play. If I can't play, then I won't get paid, then I'll lose the house, you know? It's like a chain reaction. If I lose my tone, I can't fuck, can't make love, can't do nothin'. I'll just walk into the ocean and die, if I lose my tone. And to lose it in front of an audience! That's happened, when the microphone gets unbalanced; there's too much shit on the horn and it's like playing through a piece of wood. My tone doesn't go through like that. It goes through like this." He makes a delicate pushing sound with his lips. "It's a whole segment of things that goes through your mouth and your mouthpiece and the horn and the note and the bell. For me to lose that"—he shudders slightly. "That's what I play off. My sound, and other people's sound."

MILES REMEMBERS

"My father was a dentist, and I used to work in his office all the time, making false plates. He had three degrees by the time he was twenty-four years old. He skipped high school and went straight to college. I used to look at that shit every day and think, how could he have done that—and in 1924? Anyway, I know I didn't want to sit in an office with the air conditioner.

"I remember a program on the radio—'Harlem Rhythm'—and I'd wait on that to come on. My sister took piano lessons, and across the street from my father's office, Jimmy Blanton used to play all the time.

"Black schools in St. Louis are something else, they'd

have, like, one trumpet? Two trumpets? They had a Miles Davis Day for me in St. Louis, named a school after me, a street. My teacher made a speech, he said how he told my father, '*That* one ain't gonna be no dentist.'

"When I started out I played the cornet, 'cause I was so small, and the trumpet seemed like *that*." He stretches his hands wide. "And all the other guys were big. My tone came from my instructor, Mr. Edgar Buchanan; he used to play with Andy Kirk. He had that real 'nice' sound, not too big, and guys from St. Louis played like that—Clark Terry, Harold Baker. There was a guy named Levi, too, and he was a motherfucker—but he was just crazy. They had him in an institution, but he got out periodically. Levi had Clark Terry's sound down. We had the same mouthpiece; we got it from a German teacher named Gustav, and Levi was Gustav's main pupil. He could play for the symphony, but Levi was black, so . . . no symphony for him, right?

"When big bands came to St. Louis, they knew they could pick up a trumpet player or a show drummer. When they needed one, they'd come up on the boat from New Orleans. When I was fifteen, a trumpet player named Clifford—he also taught science—called me up and said, 'Adam Lambert and his brother Famous Lambert are playing in Springfield [Illinois] and they need a trumpet player who can read, and I asked your mother if you could play and she said okay.' School was out and it was only a week's work. They gave me a hundred and ten dollars. I played with all the trumpet players in St. Louis—Eddie Brown and Bruz Roberts. He had the cutest sound. He always wanted me to play but I wanted to hear him. They'd all tell me don't play like this"—Miles imitates Dizzy Gillespie—"do like this." Miles imitates Miles. "So that's the way it was in St. Louis. You hear that and it's in your body. You can only play what you hear.

"By then all the cats had heard about me—but I didn't

know it. They were coming into clubs where Terry and I used to jam. I learned real fast, though. My father's best friend—he was a real estate broker but they'd both worked their way through college playing music—heard me practice and he brought me a book. Said, 'See this? These are chromatic scales, and you can't do nuthin' till you learn that.' " He laughs. "So I learned it overnight. Robby Danson, one of my best friends, would say, 'Check this record out,' and we'd copy the solos. When a new band came to town, we'd watch the drummer set up, and if he didn't set up right, we'd leave. Robby'd just say, 'Let's go.'

"But all the great players came through St. Louis, you see. Billy Eckstine had Bird and Dizzy. We heard Jimmie Lunceford, Freddie Webster. When McKinney's Cotton Pickers came, they offered me twenty-five dollars a night to go with them, but my mother wouldn't let me go. They came to the clubs where I was working but I didn't know till much later *why*. Illinois Jacquet came, and Howard McGhee would say, 'Go on up there.' I'd say, 'You go up!' I always wanted to hear him play. So I knew everyone before I went to New York. When I told my father I wanted to go to Juilliard, he said, 'You can go. Do what you want to do—but *good*.'

"When I got to New York, all the big bands had disbanded because it was too much money—so everyone was there. Lucky. I got Sonny Rollins, Roy Haynes, and Sonny Stitt for one audition. Sonny Rollins used to play in one of Bird's styles—until he heard Trane. Trane played like Dexter but he kept progressing. I had Trane and Sonny at the same time, and you know, we used to go up to Harlem and play these benefits where everyone would dance. I wish we had tapes of that. Trane would get down. I'd wonder, 'What is he gonna play next?' Sometimes we used Art [Blakey], sometimes Kenny Clarke. It was like going to Peru, to the gold museum.

"And nobody said 'Don't play like that' in those days. Nobody said 'jazz,' they said 'bebop.' I can't remember all that stuff, though, 'cause I never read those magazines. I did read 'em once: I won the 'new star' award in 1946 [in *Down Beat*] and that was it. Six books on me now, and I haven't read any yet.

"I gave Coltrane his first soprano saxophone, you know. We were in France, and an antique dealer there wanted to give me a trumpet. I said, 'I already have one; give me one of those things that Sidney Bechet plays.' After that he never put it down. In the bus, in the hotel . . . the sound turned him on. And the electric sound was what turned Keith [Jarrett] and Herbie [Hancock] on. It turned all of them on." He laughs. "And the rest is history.

"Cannonball and them all started using the Fender piano. We weren't copying the sound, we just liked it. Mainly because Joe [Zawinul] played so nice on the Fender. Keith played so nice I had to give him two pianos. He'd go like this." Miles imitates Jarrett in a pianistic frenzy. "I'd say, 'Keith, how does it feel to be a *genius*?'

"With the musical caliber of Joe Zawinul, it put some weight in the band—especially when you write for the bass and piano to play the same lines. I learned that from "Kleine Kammermusik," a quintet by Paul Hindemith. I found that if you had three notes and the third in the bass, it would sound larger than the tonic. For a C chord, you put the E in the bass instrument—keep the same register—and then the three parts would sound like a bass sound. It was like: pow! And people would say, 'What is that?' I'd have the score and I'd say, 'It's four notes and all of them are doubled.' What I'm saying is that you can take the 'fatness' out of the chord and get the same sound, put whatever you want on top and it's louder and fuller.

"I learned a lot of this back in 1948. It was Gil Evans and I, Gerry Mulligan, George Russell, and John Carisi. We used to read scores together and stuff. Gil and I have been friends ever since. He'd give me stuff he wanted me to hear, like Harry Partch. And Monk used to teach me. I'd say, 'What chord is that?' 'Cause with his chords you had to find the note that would make the chord and resolve it too, know where you're going. He used a lot of minor sixths, major sevenths—a lush sound.

"Now it's a little bit different, but I like it. They've taken the textures of orchestration and synthesized it: You can play with five pieces what used to take seventeen. So instead of playing against Sonny and Jackie McLean, you prerecord it on the keyboard and then lay against that. It's just another challenge.

"I liked what Marcus did for me on *Tutu*. We sequenced the drum parts because they're polyrhythmic, and Stevie [Thornton, Miles's percussionist] can't always remember them. Seems like nobody uses Afro-Cuban anymore except Miami Sound Machine. But Marcus know what sounds go better with my tone, and if you take a sample of my tone and put it in the keyboard, certain voicings will cater to your sound. I told my son, 'If you want to be a true musician, you have to be like Marcus Miller: be able to play piano, drums, bass, all of it.' That's the way it is today and I love it.

"What I used to play, with Tony Williams, Jack DeJohnette, Herbie, Chick, Cannonball, Bill Evans, all those different modes and substitute chords, we had the energy then and we liked it. But I have no feel for it anymore. Other people still do it, but it doesn't have the same spark. It's more like warmed-over turkey.

"Wynton Marsalis? I don't know about him, man. But I know he doesn't talk like that when we're alone together. 'Preserve this' and 'preserve that'—the way they're going we'll have blacks back on the plantation. I mean, it already *is* preserved. Isn't that what records are all about?

"I just tell people it's like this: I can't wear bell-bottom pants anymore. And I don't drive an Edsel. I drive a Ferrari."

THE THIRTY-YEAR ITCH

Miles is getting restless. He's not the sort to luxuriate in reminiscence—or perhaps he's just been sitting in one place for too long, which isn't his style either. He gets up and walks over to the piano, fingers a few chords, then loses interest and wanders into a small, windowless room that features a set of drums and some keyboards. "My nephew practices here," he explains. More than a dozen of Miles's paintings are casually stacked against the base of the walls, some lying on the floor. He picks up a couple and shows them to his visitor. A sketched self-portrait lies on top of the drum kit. He flips it face down before leaving the room.

He puts on a concert tape recorded in Copenhagen. The sound is lush, beautiful. It's slated to come out on Columbia, he says, his last contracted LP for the label after a relationship spanning nearly thirty years.

Why did he leave? "Different reasons. When we did this I wanted fourteen hundred dollars for a digital remix and Columbia wouldn't pay it. And then [Columbia vice-president] George Butler calls me up. He says to me, 'Why don't you call Wynton?' I say, 'Why?' He says, ' 'Cause it's his birthday.' " Miles gives a look that could wither a stone. "That's why I left Columbia."

Moments later, Miles is blasting a funky concert tape. His sister looks up from her seat on the back terrace with an expression of recognition and delight. She and Miles start making faces at each other. Miles's moods are like New England weather: variable and subject to sudden change.

When I relay Teo Macero's observation that Miles's music can be traced to the nature of his relationships to different women, he laughs disparagingly: "That has nothing to do with it. There's worse things that can happen to you than a woman, you know; things that make your heart race. Music can help that. That's why they put it in hospitals, offices, elevators—why a woman sings when she puts a child to sleep. Somebody asked me, 'What would you do if your wife left? What would happen?' And I told him, 'I'd play a B-flat major seventh, and then I'd feel all right.'"

He turns on the TV, which happens to be featuring a news program about a racially motivated attack of three black men by whites in Howard Beach, Queens, New York. Anyone who has spoken with Miles soon discovers that he's a very race-conscious (*not* racist) individual. He chooses friends and associates on their merits, but his experiences with race prejudice—including police beatings—are a lasting source of bitterness. He watches the news with grave attention, then calls his sister over. Neither speaks at first, but seem to bear witness to the account of this latest outrage. "Musically, I think things are a lot better," he says after a spell. "But you know"—he gestures toward the TV screen—"this is New York. And then the police use that electric thing [the stun gun] . . . I think some things are going to blow this summer. Almost like it has to. Terrorists aren't doing their shit for nothing."

I ask Miles if he has any personal heroes outside the music world, such as politicians who speak for him. He shakes his head no. "I listen to Jesse Jackson, Benjamin Hooks, James Baldwin, people like that. If they say the wrong thing, it just bounces off me. But I don't believe in nonviolence. It never works; they just take advantage of us.

"Not all the time, you understand. But I wouldn't sit still to see a friend hurt—be they black or white."

This last remark sounds similar to sentiments voiced recently by South African bishop Desmond Tutu, the namesake for Miles's album. He brightens up hearing the comparison. "Tutu said that?" he asks. "Well, I think we look alike."

THE IMPORTANCE OF BEING MILES

In the autumn of his years, Miles Davis would seem to have it all: fame, fortune, a seemingly solid marriage, rejuvenated health, a lifetime of creative accomplishment. Yet he appears to be entering yet another of his celebrated transitions. Within a week of the Los Angeles concerts, Miles has canned guitarist McKnight from the band, and associates predict more changes are imminent. "He's hearing a different sound," one explains. His 1987 performing schedule features concerts around the world, including a tentative State Department tour of the Soviet Union.

What drives this man? He claims that when he put down his trumpet for most of the 1970s, "it didn't bother me at all. I just didn't feel like playing. But then Dizzy came around the house and said, 'What the fuck are you doing? You were put here to play music!' For him to say that," Miles says sheepishly, "well, Dizzy's like a brother to me. So I started back."

Since his return he's continued to refine that personal synthesis of rock, funk, and jazz he pioneered in the late sixties and which devolved into "fusion" in the hands of a hundred lesser artists. But while records like *Bitches Brew* and *Jack Johnson* took their cues from Sly Stone and Jimi Hendrix, Miles's recent works are more reflective of the slick eighties pop zeitgeist. He not only performs modern ballads like "Time After Time," "Human Nature," and "Perfect Way," but goes on to express admiration for the compositional forms of bands like Scritti Politti, Nik Kershaw, and even Mister Mister. "I don't know what their women tell them," Miles cracks, "but these white guys write some beautiful ballads."

To Miles's current critics, this attitude falls somewhere between sacrilege and senility—no matter that he can make rhinestones sparkle like jewels. But his direction makes perfect sense to Miles: He's simply addressing the modern equivalents of the standards he cut his teeth on in the forties. And even the nastiest critic will acknowledge Miles's special gift for romantic interpretation.

"I think 'Time After Time' or that ballad from *Cats* will become standards, and some of the old ones will disappear," he observes. "It's been a long time for 'Body and Soul' now, forty years. There should be some turnover, don't you think? I think Prince writes great music-hall songs, like the ones they used to in Britain. Prince's are a little different, though," he admits. "Like the one about the girl in the lobby with the magazine—you know that one?" Prince holds a special place in Miles's personal pantheon. Rumors abound about possible collaborations between them, especially now that both are connected to Warner Bros. Records. Miles shrugs off inquiries, but adds: "He wrote me a letter and said, 'You gotta hang out with me and Sheila E., 'cause a lot of people have to find out who you are.' And then he signed it, 'God.' "

That cracks Miles up. "He is so talented. I can't say enough about him." One gets the feeling Miles senses a lot of himself in young "God." If Prince keeps up his current level of productivity for thirty more years, Miles might turn out to be right.

For the present, however, Miles evidently enjoys his privileges. He's become more relaxed in public, he says, "because people recognize that I am what I am. But the reason I'm getting more respect now," he goes on, "is because of television. It's really 'Miami Vice' and the Honda commercial—that's the truth. You know, if we do a concert in France that gets shown on national television. Here, the only way a black person gets on TV is like this." He mimics a suspect getting frisked. "It's sad."

Then Miles remembers something, and his expression softens. "This woman brought her little boy to a show, and the whole time he just looked at me like this," Miles says, widening his eyes into saucers. "Just stared at me. I said to the woman, 'Why don't you buy him a Casio?' She said, 'I did that. He just wants to play trumpet.' So I said to him, 'Okay, let me see your teeth.' He kept looking at me. 'Well, maybe you can play trumpet if you don't suck your thumb. You gotta wait a couple of years, though. You're still too young even to hold a trumpet.'

"He just kept staring at me, never let his eyes go. So I said, 'All right. I'll teach you when you grow up.' "

—*March 1987*

JOHN COLTRANE:

A LIFE SUPREME

BY PETER

WATROUS

■

John Coltrane died in 1967,

twenty years ago this summer. America had seen the

rise and assassination of Malcolm X and was about to

experience Martin Luther King's death. It was more

than just dancing in the streets; there was a riot going

on, perhaps the greatest urban turmoil in the country's

history. The arts were in upheaval, too: The Beatles

were finishing Sgt. Pepper's *and reshaping notions of*

pop; the Grand Union, a New York school of dance

including Twyla Tharp and Merce Cunningham, were

using improvisation and random motion; junk and pop art were replacing the established abstract expressionists. There was a rupture with the past going on, in other words, and John Coltrane, who'd started out as a saxophonist deep in the jazz traditions, was one of its leaders.

In a sense he is the archetypal sixties artist, the man who reshaped the iconography of the jazz genius from the brilliant burnout of Charlie Parker—a fifties beat idea—to that of the abstaining saint, paradoxically meditative and angry, Eastern and American. He became the paradigm of the searching artist. Though it can be argued that Coltrane helped end jazz's mass popularity with his expressionistic, visceral approach to music, his own appeal and influence were immense, reaching beyond the confines of jazz or even music. And after two subsequent decades of often jarring cultural and political cynicism, his trademarks of honesty, forthrightness, and an overwhelming desire to change, to do things that haven't been done before, seem more than just appealing—they seem necessary.

For me, Coltrane's astounding emotional power comes from his sound, that chillingly personal cry that's his identity, the one note that can be heard from his fumbling, early recordings with Dizzy Gillespie to the last dates five months before he died. It's not a warm or a friendly sound; it's simply a fact that carries with it an indifference to acceptability. To me Coltrane has always sounded lonely, a three A.M. blue wail that gives succor and sympathy to those in trouble. There's passion in everything he played, even the hundreds of blowing sessions he tossed off to remind us what it means to be alive. You feel his rawness, his lack of equivocation, his honesty.

Coltrane was a natural. He also worked extremely hard at cultivating his talent. He didn't "do" anything in a Hollywood sense: His life reflects an almost monastic dedication to learning and to advancing, both as a musician and as a person. The son of a tailor and grandchild of two ministers (his mother's father, also a state senator, was known for fire-and-brimstone sermons) grew up in High Point, North Carolina, in what passed for the black aristocracy. In school he played alto sax in Reverend Steele's Community Band. By the time he graduated from high school in 1943, he already exhibited the sort of aloofness that made him seem mysterious—actually, he was shy—and he was known as *the* musician in High Point.

In 1944 Coltrane moved to Philadelphia and began his fanatical practice routine, from ten to twelve hours a day. Following a navy stint, he joined an R&B band led by Joe Webb and featuring the great blues shouter Big Maybelle, then twenty-two, who loved Coltrane's tone. He went to California as part of Eddie "Cleanhead" Vinson's group, where he met and played with his idol, Charlie Parker. Vinson wanted Coltrane as a tenor player, not an altoist; the change of instruments allowed him to move away from Parker's influence. "On tenor," said Coltrane, "I found there was no one man whose ideas were so dominant. I listened to almost all the good tenor men, beginning with Lester, and believe me, I've picked up something from all of them, including several who haven't recorded."

SONNY ROLLINS

I first heard him in a band with Kenny Clarke. I remember very well. John and Kenny, it was fantastic. And I recall thinking that John was a puzzle. I could never figure out how he arrived at, how he came up with, what he played. It was one of the things that made him unique. I never got a better fix on it through the years. Like any genius, it's hard to get a handle on how they come up with their ideas.

His influence was very pervasive. But I don't think it's necessarily bad to have influences. It's inevitable. Any guy

*who's that much into music is bound to be listening heavily
to someone before him, like I did with Coleman Hawkins.
The individuality will come out if it's there. It depends
whether or not the individual player can transcend the influence. To play what we call modern music, you need some
antecedents.*

*Although he had a sense of humor, he was quite serious
most of the time. Almost like a guy who would be a minister,
especially about music. You realized you were in the presence of someone who held the sacred in high regard. His
humor wasn't about cracking jokes or anything like that,
he was more droll or wry.*

*I remember when I heard the news of his death. I was
working somewhere and I took some people back to Brooklyn. In those days we wouldn't get out of the clubs until four
in the morning. By the time I got back home it was light out.
I was listening to WOR and there was a quote from Elvin to
the effect that John never hurt anybody. It was a shock; I
had just talked to him two weeks earlier. We were always
close.*

Postwar Philadelphia was musically fertile; clubs were
everywhere, and since the city was on the black tour circuit, local people were often picked up by big-name
groups. "Philadelphia was a mecca for bebop," says saxophonist Jimmy Heath, a soft-spoken man who was one of
Coltrane's best friends. "There was a lot of jamming going
on; everybody was trying to learn. It was a family type
of affair." That year Miles Davis blew into town; having
recorded with Charlie Parker's group, he wasn't quite a
star but his style was already well-known.

"I heard Trane in Philadelphia," says Miles Davis.
"When he picked up the tenor, his eyes were on Dexter
and Sonny Stitt. I used to have him and Sonny Rollins in
the same band, and Art Blakey. That was a *baad* band I

had, *goddamn*! So he started working with me. I got him and Philly Joe. And Paul Chambers. He was playing, you know, like Dexter, kicking out different long phrases. I *loved* when he would do that, when he would imitate, like Eddie Davis. It was so funny."

Heroin was endemic to the jazz community of the time; it was cheap, and the long-term effects of addiction hadn't yet become obvious. Coltrane, twenty-two, was fitting in. "There were a lot of guys that were messed up on drugs," says Sonny Rollins, "but I never looked at John in that way. He was never that type of guy. It's incongruous. But I guess it happened, and at times he was messed up. It was out of character." To support himself, Coltrane would play R&B dates around the city, walking the bar and honking. "We all had to walk the bar," says Heath. "That was the fad of the time. People would throw money in the bell of your horn. John could adapt to it, but that wasn't his forte, there was too much repetition, the 'Flying Home' type solos." One night Benny Golson entered a club just as Coltrane was stalking the bar. Embarrassed, Coltrane jumped off the bar, walked out the door, and never came back.

Nineteen fifty-five, when Charlie Parker died, was also the year Miles Davis put together his first famous quintet, with Philly Joe Jones, Paul Chambers, Red Garland, and Coltrane. John had been working a two-week stint with organist Jimmy Smith, who asked him to join when Philly Joe called him to make a date with Miles. The same week, Coltrane married Naima Grubbs, after whom he would name two songs. She was both traditionally religious (a Muslim) and into astrology, interests Coltrane himself would pursue for the rest of his life.

The Miles Davis group of 1955 set the course for jazz over the next five years. The two horn players, though rooted in bop, took idiosyncratic approaches to its language, Miles by distilling the essence of a phrase into a few notes, Coltrane by cramming bushels of them into a small harmonic space. His early playing with Miles seems slightly out of control; snatches of undigested Dexter Gordon and Sonny Stitt float by and Coltrane's lines come at you in all directions, sputtering one moment, graceful the next. But he has the "it" Jack Kerouac wrote about: the sound, the excitement and unpredictability of blowing, the way he puts together notes, the way he's thinking about what phrase makes sense next to what phrase. Mark him, Miles would say to Coltrane's critics, as someone who is finding his own way.

He was starting to record frequently: a Davis date in late 1955 (*New Miles Davis Quintet*), with Elmo Hope for Prestige in 1956, and the *Tenor Madness* date with Sonny Rollins, a legendary matchup of the up-and-coming tenorists.

The session, their only recorded meeting, came about by accident. "John went out to the date with us," says Sonny Rollins with characteristic offhandedness, "because in those days a lot of musicians hung out together. There were more friendships; people would be immersed in music twenty-four hours a day. You'd be over at somebody's house listening to records for days at a time. John was either with Red Garland or Philly Joe Jones, I believe. Money wouldn't have entered it. John had asked me right after that period to make another record together. Much to my regret, we never did."

Much was made about tensions between the two top young tenor saxophonists of the time. Rollins, who considered Coltrane one of his closest friends, never saw it that way. "It was hard to be competitive with John, because he was bigger than that, his playing and his person. We were competitive in musical terms, sure, to a degree. I think all guys are judged by who's around you. But I don't think he spent a lot of time trying to consciously compete with other people."

By 1956, Coltrane's drug and drinking problems had worsened; he was looking bad onstage and using up all his money. In St. Louis, Paul Chambers and Coltrane checked out of their hotel via the window. Miles disbanded the group. "He was no trouble," says Miles. "But when he was there he used to say [in a hurt tone], 'You never talk to us.' Well, 'You never sober up enough for me to talk to you.' "

Back in New York, Coltrane was still drinking heavily and playing badly, and bassist Reggie Workman confronted him about it. He went off the bottle, but after three days his thought patterns had screwed up and he couldn't speak properly. He stayed in his house for about two weeks, prayed a lot, then woke up one day without the urge for a drink. "The person who gets all the credit for helping him to clean up is Naima," says Workman. "She's the one who stayed with him through everything and helped him clear his life."

Nineteen fifty-seven was the turning point in Coltrane's odyssey, a watershed that only an extremely disciplined person could effect. He set up schedules for studying, practicing, listening to other players. He had a dream, the second actually, in which Charlie Parker came to him (in the first, Parker had told him to give up alto) and suggested he "keep on those progressions 'cause that's the right thing to do."

Prestige Records, not known for its largesse to musicians, offered Coltrane a contract in March 1957, and he began to record regularly (at least thirteen dates in '57 alone, including *Dakar*, his first as a leader). Critics, who for the most part hadn't liked what Coltrane was playing, soon realized he'd achieved a profound mastery of his instrument, that he was crossing musical frontiers. He came in second in the New Star category in *Down Beat*, recorded the well-received *Blue Train*, and, most importantly joined Monk for his legendary gig at the Five Spot in New York, which drew audiences beyond jazz circles, including painters Franz Kline and Willem de Kooning; the latter called Coltrane "an Einstein of music."

The difference from his tentative solos with Miles the year before is astonishing. A marvel of technique, he started experimenting with different ways to approach the same chords. On *Blue Train* he played hot and fast, a sort of hyper-bopper, draping the changes with waves of notes. By now he'd shed his influences and was deep into harmony, superimposing chord on chord, creating a sheen critic Ira Gitler would name "sheets of sound." He was working on multiphonics, which he'd learned from saxophonist John Glenn and from Monk. Intrigued by harp music, he would check the paper for Marx Brothers movies, and persistently asked Naima to take up the instrument.

Coltrane rejoined Miles at the end of the year; the group now featured Bill Evans on piano, Cannonball Adderly on alto and a book that used modes as a way to simplify harmonic movement. It was completely antithetical to what Coltrane was working on at the time—the superimposition of chords, dense harmonic webs—yet he fit in perfectly, using the harmonic spaces to experiment with all the chord substitutions he was thinking about. Miles places Coltrane's development: "I said, 'Trane, you can play these chords against the tonic of another chord,' and he was the only one who could do it. Lucky Thompson, maybe. Plus, when I did *Milestones*, with Bill Evans, I wrote out these little things for Trane, these little things within a mode, to see what he could do on them. It was always a challenge for him. The chords I showed him were just like dominant chords against dominant chords, a minor, diminished and half step . . . he could play that in one chord and the trick is, not the trick, but to play them so you can hear the sound of the chord you're playing against. It's always a challenge if you're up in the air, because you're tired of the suspended diminished chord after everything. It's like not having an orgasm, but holding it in."

By late 1958 Coltrane had become a big enough star to leave Prestige and ask for a thousand-dollar advance per album. Not only was he playing with Miles Davis, which was placing him in front of audiences beyond jazz fans, he was becoming a figure of controversy, acknowledged to be doing something different.

Coltrane's own commitment had gotten to the point where he'd take the saxophone to the dinner table with him, fall asleep in bed with the reed in his mouth. He'd practice until he couldn't play anymore, sometimes for twenty-four hours straight. One result was *Giant Steps*, recorded in May 1959, an album that seemed to put an end at the time to the possibilities of chord changes. The title composition sounds like the sort of complicated exercise music students write for themselves to help master chordal playing. Coltrane sounds mechanical; the tune reinforces his occasional rhythmic stiffness. Still, the record is rightly considered a masterpiece. Partly it's the writing—listen to the stunning forthrightness of "Cousin Mary"—and partly Coltrane's assertive, startling playing.

"I was living on 101st and Coltrane was on 103rd Street," pianist Tommy Flanagan recalls. "He came by my apartment with this piece, 'Giant Steps.' I guess he thought there was something different about it, because he sat down and played the changes. He said, 'It's no problem. I know you can do it, Maestro'—which is what he called me. 'If I can play this, you can.' There *was* no problem just looking at the changes. But I didn't realize he was going to play it at that *tempo!* There was no time to shed on it, there was no melody; it was just a set of chords, like we usually get. So we ran it down and we had maybe one take, because he played marvelous on everything. He was ready. As he said later on, the whole date was tunes he wanted to get out of his system. He was using that sequence in the bridge."

ORNETTE COLEMAN

He called me up and asked if I would join his band. I was very interested in trying to get the things I was playing in the public's eye, but I was having too much trouble with the business, so I hadn't been out in clubs for a long time. I thought I'd better go out and see what's going on. When I went to the Vanguard, Max Gordon called me over and said, "Somebody just canceled—could you bring in a band?" And that's the only thing that stopped me from joining Coltrane.

In the early Sixties he was studying with me. He was interested in nonchordal playing, and I had cut my teeth on that stuff. He later sent me a letter which included thirty dollars for each lesson, and thanked me. [That influence] showed up very clearly because all of a sudden a guy who had been playing very "legitimately" started playing strictly from his own spiritual and emotional state without worrying about his past. Had he lived, Trane would probably have legitimized that concept. I thought he had a beautiful tone. I thought it was very humane.

I thought it ["Body and Soul"] went down very smooth. "Giant Steps" was just a part of three songs he was to use called Suite Sioux. *One was based on "Cherokee." It was one of the ones we really didn't get, it posed too much of a problem. It was still at that tempo, and it was supposed to go from "Giant Steps" to "Suite Sioux," to "Countdown," which I think was faster yet. Paul [Chambers] had no solo on those pieces, but just keeping up with the sequence of the chords was hard, they were going down fast.*

I had no idea [how influential the date would become]. A date with Trane, you knew it was going to be important. It seemed like years later people started saying, "What was it like?" It was like any other date to me. It was a date.

"We had rehearsed at my mother's house in Harlem," says Arthur Taylor, the drummer on the session. "He wanted to rehearse with me before the date. So he brought his horn. We just ran over the pieces for about half an hour or so, and he left.

"I don't put that much importance on the record myself. I've done better records than that with Coltrane. It still remains a heck of a document, people all around the world look to that, and musicians also; that's the thing. I don't like the sound of it. John was very serious, like a magician too. He was serious and we just got down to the business at hand."

Ironically, *Giant Steps* ended Coltrane's dense approach to harmony. *Kind of Blue*, Miles Davis's masterpiece of modality, was recorded at the same time, with Coltrane playing an integral part. Coltrane absorbed a lot of knowledge through mentors—Miles and Monk are just two examples. By late 1959, he was talking with Sun Ra about recording together. Soon after that he began to play the soprano saxophone.

He'd increased his reading to include books on art, music theory, African history, physics, math, anthropology. His record collection had music from Africa, Afghanistan, Russia, France, early England, Greece, American Indians, India, Arabia and all types of black American music. "He was into Indian music and into African music, and different social groups," says McCoy Tyner, the pianist who charted the idiosyncratic harmonic sound of the classic Coltrane quartet of the sixties. "On 'Dahomey Dance' [from *Olé*], he had a record of these guys who were from Dahomey, which is why he used two bassists. He showed that rhythm to Art Davis and Reggie Workman. So the influence was there."

By 1960 it was time to leave Miles Davis's group and head out on his own. A live recording from March of that year, done in Europe during Coltrane's last tour with Davis, finds him straitjacketed by Jimmy Cobb's drumming. His intensely detailed, whirling lines seem to be seeking the more mutable, interactive drumming he'd find with Elvin Jones, and a less rigid context for improvisation. On "Green Dolphin Street" he reduces the tune to nothing, unleashing torrents of notes that obliterate the changes.

Giant Steps was well received, and after returning from the European tour, Coltrane gave Miles two weeks' notice. The owners of the Five Spot (the club that had presented Monk and Coltrane three years earlier) now ran a club called the Jazz Gallery; they offered him a twenty-week engagement, which shows their appraisal of his drawing power. Coltrane put his first quartet together for the gig: drummer Pete La Rocca, Steve Kuhn on piano, and Philadelphia bassist Steve Davis. The first set of the first night, during a Coltrane solo, a bald man dressed in a loincloth ran up to the stage yelling "Coltrane, Coltrane," followed by Monk. Though Coltrane left after nine weeks, the stay was hugely successful, with Ravi Shankar, Cecil Taylor and others coming by to listen. Coltrane quickly fired Kuhn and La Rocca, replacing them with McCoy Tyner and Elvin Jones (whom Coltrane had wanted anyway). In a few months Steve Davis was replaced by Reggie Workman, who later gave way to Jimmy Garrison, and the quartet found its sound for the next four years.

He invited me to his house after we met and said he wanted to get together with me because we were play-ing . . . not the same way, but in the same areas of the horn. He said, "You're playing some funny stuff." He wanted to sit down and talk about it. He was playing the piano mostly, I think it was the beginning of "Giant Steps," those aug-mented thirds over and over. He'd get his horn and play two notes for a long time. Then two others, then two others. We also talked about doing impossible things with your instrument. We also talked about starting a sentence in the middle, and then going to the beginning and the end of it at the same time.

George Tucker, the bassist, would come by, Cedar Wal-ton too. Freddie Hubbard. John would ask me to spend the night. That happened more than once. We'd cook food. Then he came to Jersey to my parents' house, on Thanksgiving. He'd talk with [Albert] Ayler, he liked him. He wanted to check out what was going on with the scene. Not just tenor, but flute and other things; I think that's why he grabbed that bagpipe toward the end. It was all-encompassing. Charlie Parker was realizing that before he died too.

From 1955 on, he had a sense of urgency. Like he couldn't get everything he wanted out. I think Trane knew something about his health, even if he couldn't pin it down.

I think one of John's legacies is that any melody has a flexibility beyond what it initially seems. Nothing is frozen. He said that everything can be opened up but it's a lot of work. There are people who say you've got to do "Nature Boy" just the way it is. And the "Star Spangled Banner." Hey, you can really take the "Star Spangled Banner" out!

Coltrane ran his groups like Miles Davis had his, with-out interfering. They rehearsed a total of six or seven times during McCoy Tyner's entire tenure. "He was a great leader," says Tyner. "Never self-imposing. I loved working for him. He was more like a brother. I had a chance to develop. Just playing and listening to him every night and creating something underneath him and creating our own thing when it came time, was quite challenging for a young guy.

"Never did he say how to play piano. He was just not that kind of person. He picked people he didn't have to do that with. Which I thought was very, very smart."

My Favorite Things, his next release for Atlantic, brought Coltrane his widest recognition. Here he embraced the modality he'd learned with Miles Davis, but turned the stark impressionism of Miles's approach into extroverted intensity; his novel treatment of the title track laid the groundwork for the next five years, until the radically different *Ascension*. Completely unlike anything Coltrane, Davis, or anybody, had done, *Things* still swings in a loose, open way. Harmonic vistas open, Coltrane sounds relaxed, his soprano sax wafting over the pliant background—the fury and impatience of his playing with Miles has been assuaged by a group whose rhythmic liberties match his own.

Just how empathetic the group became is spelled out by Tyner, who remembers one night in the early sixties when Miles tried to sit in at Birdland. "There wasn't any room. He didn't quite work. We were very special. It was very difficult for anybody to walk up and come into the band."

GREG OSBY

People still romanticize that stereotype of a strung-out musician not in control of his life. Coltrane was one of the first to rise above. He studied, he implemented new ideas, his business was together. That's why he represents, to me, somebody in control of his destiny.

I heard him when I was still listening to funk, I guess it was around 1974. I hadn't been playing more than two years, but I was listening to Coltrane, playing my funk licks on top of "Giant Steps." I didn't know what he was doin', or any harmonies, or any of his musical logic, but I could enjoy it; I know it was "bad," and one day I wanted to get with that.

That's what jazz is about; you're supposed to be versatile, derive from other sources, I mean alien sources. I hear some players today who are so conservative they could be on Reagan's staff.

LEO SMITH

He was a train that pulled a lot with him. He tried, in every place, to show people what he really saw. And he wasn't afraid to take young players and lead them. Many players have been unwilling to do that. A lot of people put fashion between them. And of course the spiritual connotation and properties of music; no one talked about those things before he came around. That was a big influence for Albert Ayler and many other people of the day. At home I listen to "Dear Lord" or A Love Supreme, Africa Brass, Om, Ascension: *those are the ones I often return to.*

Once, with Miles, when Coltrane explained he didn't know how to stop soloing, Davis suggested that he take the saxophone out of his mouth. Now his tunes were getting longer—between an hour or two in live performance. Nonetheless, *My Favorite Things* went gold—almost unheard of in jazz—and *Newsweek* covered Coltrane's weeklong stay in July at the Village Vanguard. Eric Dolphy joined the group that summer and they recorded *Africa Brass* for Impulse, a gorgeous, agitated big-band album arranged by Dolphy and Tyner.

Coltrane's next record, *Live at the Village Vanguard*, featured "Chasin' the Trane," a long blues named by engineer Rudy Van Gelder (who had a tough time tracking Coltrane's horn for the recording) that caused outrage among critics and listeners, inciting a double review, pro and con, in *Down Beat*. "Chasin' the Trane" is one of the magnificent recordings of jazz. It begins with a simple opening melody and gradually, maintaining the same level of emotionality, grows more complex. Coltrane starts blowing harmonics, raising the ante; McCoy Tyner keeps out of the way, and especially stunning is the way Coltrane and Elvin Jones reinvent straight-ahead 4/4 swing, turning the tune into a tumultuous event.

"He was very much a man of conviction," notes Art Davis, one of Coltrane's favorite bassists, "even though a lot of people said a lot of very bad, hurting things about him. He'd say, 'That's their opinion,' rather than cursing someone out or saying, 'If I see that motherfucker, I'm going to beat the shit out of him.' "

Coltrane had six years to live from the time he made *Africa Brass*. He recorded an astounding twenty-five albums in that time (not counting the alternate takes and snippets that began to surface after his death); their overall quality virtually unparalleled. After *Live at the Village Vanguard* came a series of albums that took his oceanic modalism to its limits. *Impressions* (the title track is based on the minimal harmony of Miles Davis's "So What") and *Coltrane* led into three dates which were suggested by Impulse: *Ballads, Duke Ellington and John Coltrane* and *John Coltrane With Johnny Hartman*.

Bob Thiele, Coltrane's producer, pretty much gave him

the keys to the studio, to the point of risking his job. "To the best of my recollection, Coltrane had a contract that called for two albums a year. Well, hell, we recorded six albums a year. And I was always brought on the carpet because they couldn't understand why I was spending the money. Most of the critics and the various music magazines were putting Coltrane down. And there's one time I did suggest to him, 'Why don't we just go in and show these guys.' I suggested we do an album of popular songs, which became *Ballads*, a beautiful album, and he loved it. And that started to turn the critics around."

By 1962 and 1963, the radical edge was beginning to show in records and American society. Civil rights leader Medgar Evers was murdered in his garage; in Birmingham, Alabama, four girls were killed when a black church was bombed. Bob Dylan released "The Times They Are a Changin' " as the folk movement was aligning itself with the political New Left. Coltrane recorded what may be his most overtly political composition, "Alabama," in memory of the children killed in the church bombing, and based on the cadences of Martin Luther King's speech about the tragedy.

Politics were integral to being black and a jazz musician—they were integral to the time. Acquaintances could read various meanings into Coltrane's character because he was shy, or political connotations into his music because he rarely clarified himself. These assumptions often have to do with what part of Coltrane's life people knew him from, though they also underscore how Coltrane was accepted by different generations. "He was not involved in politics," says Milt Jackson, who was with Coltrane in Dizzy Gillespie's group and appeared on Coltrane's first Atlantic album. "I can't draw any parallels between the social times of the Sixties and John's playing," says Sonny Rollins, "though it may be relevant to somebody that grew up in the Sixties and heard Coltrane in the Sixties, and was into whatever movements were going on at the time."

Rashied Ali, who worked with Coltrane from 1965 to the end, sees it differently. "The younger people embraced the music; the older Coltrane fans, the people who dug the Coltrane from Miles Davis and the Coltrane from the early Sixties, they sort of stepped back because they couldn't get with the change. But the connection was there. He wrote songs like 'Reverend King' and 'Alabama'; that whole movement affected everybody. It affected his thinking and his thoughts about what was happening, and the music started getting rougher and tougher. Coltrane wasn't the type of person to speak out about it. But he was playing and writing music about it. And he admired people like King and Malcolm X. He kept up with things."

In an interview with writer Frank Kofsky, Coltrane put it like this: "In my opinion, I would say yes [that jazz is opposed to the United States's involvement in Vietnam] because jazz to me . . . is an expression of higher ideals. So therefore brotherhood is there; and I believe with brotherhood, there would be no poverty. And also, with brotherhood, there would be no war."

MARTY EHRLICH

Besides his incredible popularity and meaning to people who listen to jazz and black culture in general, he also commanded the attention of many people who didn't listen to jazz. It's interesting because he wasn't a commercial artist in the sense of someone reaching across boundaries today; his was a very serious and at times difficult music. A lot of that had to do with the times. His music certainly reflected the energy of the Sixties. I've found an interesting parallel between him and Béla Bartók: people who didn't listen to contemporary music often listened to Bartók. Both were innovative, expanded the language of their idiom, but at the same time used traditional folk materials a lot in their music. Radical conservatives. They grabbed you intellectually and emotionally in a way that not much music achieves. A Love Supreme *was a gold record; it's very hard to think of a record of that intensity being a gold record. But people wanted a bit more seriousness in music during that time. In that sense he was an example of what a committed musical artist could be.*

I like all his stuff. At the end of his life, like on Expression, *you can hear new areas of time along with very beautiful harmonic motion. Consistent, definitely; maybe a little bit obsessive. We hear the long solos and we're used to shorter forms these days.*

He could've stopped at any point, like in the late Fifties, and still had a career as one of the top saxophonists. But he didn't. Playing in the same language for many years allows you great conviction, but it's harder when you're trying to find new things, because how do you ever know? You can't be sure. That made his music so intense. You could feel that musical and personal discovery. His music was really about what you should do in your own music, not just keep playing A Love Supreme.

The issues that Malcolm X talked about "are definitely important," Erlich went on. "And as I said, the issues are part of what is at the time. So naturally, as musicians, we express whatever is. Well, I tell you for myself, I make a conscious attempt; I think I can truthfully say that I make, or I have tried to make, a conscious attempt to change what I've found, in music. In other words, I've tried to say, 'Well, this could be better, in my opinion, so I will try to do this to make it better.' We must make an effort. It's the same socially, musically, politically, and in any department of our lives."

In fact, Coltrane's main extra musical stimulation came not from politics but from religion. Deeply influenced by his family background, he maintained an interest in God all his life, exploring different religions, though never settling down and becoming part of one denomination. He was interested in astrology as well; the titles of some of his compositions—"Psalm," "Song of Praise," "Ascension," "Dear Lord," "Dearly Beloved," "Amen," "Attaining," "Ascent," "Cosmos," "Om," "The Father and the Son and the Holy Ghost," "Compassion," "Love Consequences," "Serenity," "Meditations," "Leo," "Mars," "Venus," "Jupiter," "Saturn"—tell the story.

By 1963, Coltrane was becoming involved with younger musicians, who saw him as a father figure of the "New Thing": Archie Shepp (who was to play on a lost version of *A Love Supreme* a year later), George Braith, Albert and Don Ayler, Bill Dixon and others. He'd separated from Naima and taken up with Alice McLeod, whom he'd later marry. His interest in the spiritual continued unabated; *A Love Supreme*, released in December of 1964, included liner notes describing his religious awakening. The album won *Down Beat*'s Record of the Year award, Coltrane was voted jazzman of the year, elected to the Hall of Fame, and won first place on tenor saxophone. The hagiography was well underway.

For many, Coltrane was the mirror reflecting their dreams or virtues. Withdrawn, quiet, he exuded an air of serenity. His personal habits—rigorous practice, vegetarianism, dabbling in odd religions—fit the times, suggesting a sort of monk looking for salvation in art. He was completely honest in his dealings with people. "I liked him because he was a musician and a serious person," says

Sonny Rollins, "almost a religious person. He had a nice unassuming quality to him. This to me was about as good as you can get in this life. As far as his personality goes, he had everything that I think was the best. He was looking for dignity. And respect as a human being. He didn't seem to be interested in self-aggrandizement. He was very young and he was just trying to get out all that music." His effect on younger musicians was more direct. "To be honest," remembers Rashied Ali, "Coltrane changed my whole concept of playing music. He made me want to play a freer, more searching type of music. I started broadening my scope of listening; it was like a refreshing breeze.

"He was kinda cool because he would be so shy," says Ali, who got to know the less formidable Coltrane. "Because he was such a great artist, people never really found out how the man was. They would say to me, 'Should I speak to him?' and they'd stand there dumbfounded, not knowing what to say. They'd ask me, 'Will you say something to him?' and I'd say, 'Why don't you go over there yourself?' All they had to do was say 'Hello,' because the guy was ready to talk, he was just a real down-home, country-type guy. Loved to laugh, loved sweet potato pie, collard greens, stuff like that. He was really what you would call a soul brother, he didn't have any weird stuff about him. He was an all right cat, the type of a person you can really call a friend."

DAVID BOWIE (ALTO SAX)

I think he undoubtedly was an influence on my wanting to play music, not ever considering that I could ever approach that kind of playing. Just for perversity's sake, I particularly used to like Eric Dolphy and Roland Kirk. When you're young, it's like one-upmanship. So many kids really liked John Coltrane, of the guys I knew who liked jazz, that

I had to push myself into "Well, who else is around that I can identify with?" [laughs] I guess Kirk really ran away with it in the end, especially during that period when he was with Mingus. But obviously Coltrane was absolutely superlative. I can't say anything of any weight about him that I'm sure half a dozen other people wouldn't say better.

He would do things for people. So many musicians were damn near living off Trane. Guys would just call him up and say, "I'm not working" or "I'm broke" or "I need this, I need that," and he'd send them a money order. He paid people's rent for them, anything he could do. He wasn't stupid, but he was definitely there if you needed him. He was just like a regular person who liked to laugh a lot.

Coltrane broke through to another level with *Ascension*, a large group date recorded in 1965 that essentially did away with regular pulsed meter and signaled Coltrane's interest in both density and musical simplicity. Unlike *Giant Steps*, the people on the date knew it was a momentous musical occasion. "When he said that it was very important," remember Art Davis, "I didn't doubt him. I didn't know what directions he was going. When I saw these people—I knew some of them, and others I didn't know— I knew ... something's important here. When I heard it, *that* was convincing."

A month later, in September, Coltrane added Pharoah Sanders to his group, and along with Donald Garret, he recorded *Om* under the influence of LSD. Two weeks later came *Kulu Se Mama*, and on the next date *Meditations*. With the addition of Rashied Ali on drums, Coltrane continued the forward motion he'd begun with *Ascension*. This ever-ballooning ensemble caused problems, however; conflict between Rashied Ali and Elvin Jones pushed the volume up and up. Then Jones left, as did McCoy Tyner, replaced by pianist/harpist Alice Coltrane.

"At the beginning we were doing the tunes Trane was famous for, 'My Favorite Things,' 'Impressions,' " says Ali. "After a while he started writing new music for the band, and that's when I started playing drums in the band alone. It was a whole different change in the music; very spiritual, and sometimes very harsh on the listeners who had been into Trane previously. Because his whole style changed."

"I really thought it was a bit too much sometimes," remembers Tyner. "I really did. I couldn't hear what I was doing. I'd look around and about five saxes would be on-stage. Where did these guys come from? Norman Simmons, who was working opposite us with Carmen McRae, said to me, 'Man, that F sharp's the sharpest note up there, really out of tune, horrible.' And I said 'Really? I can't hear it.' I could not hear my instrument. So I said, 'Well, it's time for me to exit.' "

In February and March 1967, Coltrane went into the studio for the last times. The result was *Expression*, yet another new direction. Spare, mostly calm and rhythmless, it sounds as if Coltrane had reached a level of contentment. The music displays neither the exploratory fervor of his earlier Sixties works nor the technique of his music of the late Fifties. With *Expression* and *Interstellar Space* (a duet with Ali), Coltrane had reached, through enormous self-discipline and dedication, his last plateau. In July 1967 he died of liver cancer.

It's extraordinary for anybody to have attempted this kind of odyssey, from junky bebopper to Sixties experimentalist and cultural icon. It's also extraordinary that he even mattered: A less musical person would have been bogged down by the programmatics of his art. But he did matter, and the question remains: What does he mean to us now?

One of the unfortunate things that happened to Coltrane's music in the seventies was the assimilation of his style into the mainstream. All pianists played like McCoy Tyner, all saxophonists worked Coltrane's pentatonic flurries, and they all helped reduce his music's potency. The effects he'd used to elicit certain emotional responses were out of place; in the America of Gerald Ford, where complacency was the rule, Coltrane's sounds were out of context. But his time is coming around again; at a time when the New Acquisitiveness is showing its bankruptcy, John Coltrane's music sounds real, functional again. The beautiful fury has walls to crush.

What we can glean from Coltrane is his steadfast dedication to learning and personal dignity. He absorbed knowledge so he could change, so he could eradicate the clichéd and stale. His honesty lets us know it's possible to keep going; his music can be heard as inspiration. In his dedication to ideas we can imagine our own capacities. It's an old jazz virtue, but it applies.

"When there's something you don't understand, you have to go humbly to it," Coltrane once said. "You don't go to school and sit down and say, 'I know what you're getting ready to teach me.' You sit there and you learn. You open your mind. You absorb. But you have to be quiet, you have to be still."

—July 1987

JACO

■

What can I say about Jaco?

When I first met him he was extremely present tense and, I would have to say for lack of a better term, extremely sage. He was so accepting of everything going on around him; at the same time he was arrogant and challenging: "I'm the baddest!" He was so alert, so involved in the moment. When people are in that state they're generally fun to be with. He was very alive.

The first time he came in, I had never heard him play. I forget who recommended him. Everybody'd heard my lament about the trouble I was having. I was trying to find a certain sound on the bottom end, going against the vogue at the time. It's very difficult to buck a vogue. Bass players were playing with dead strings; you couldn't get them to change to get a round, full-bodied tone. I liked that old analog, jukebox, Fifties sound—upright bass, boomier. In the Sixties and early Seventies you had this dead, distant bass sound. I didn't care for it. And the other thing was, I had started to think, "Why couldn't the bass leave the bottom sometimes and go up and play in the midrange and then return?" Why did it have to always play the root? On "The Jungle Line" I had played some kind of keyboard bass line, and when it came around to Max Bennett having to play it, he just hated it. Because sometimes it didn't root the chord, it went up into the middle. To him that was flat-out wrong. To some people it was eccentric. So when Jaco came in, John Guerin said to me, "God, you must love this guy; he almost never plays the root!"

There was a time when Jaco and I first worked together when there was nobody I'd rather hang with than him. There was an appreciation, a joie de vivre, a spontaneity. A lot of people couldn't take him. Maybe that's my peculiarity, but then, I also have a fondness for derelicts.

He had this wide, fat swath of a sound. There weren't a lot of gizmos you could put your instrument through then, and the night I got my Roland Jazz Chorus amp, it was sort of a prototype. Jaco and Bobbye Hall and I were playing a benefit up in San Francisco. I tried playing through this thing and Jaco flipped for it. So he stole it off me! He said, "Oh yeah, I'm playing through that tonight!" I said, "What are you talking about? This is my new amp!" He pointed to his rental amp and said, "I'm not playing through that piece of shit." So he took mine! We went out onstage that night and Jaco got this huge wonderful bushy sound and I played through this peanut. He was formidable! You can hear it in the mixes back then. He was very dominating. But I put up with it; I even got a kick out of it. Because I was so thrilled about the way he played. It was exactly what I was waiting for.

He was an innovator. First of all, he was changing the bottom end of the time, and he knew it. With that went a certain amount of confidence, which at its worst was offensive to some people. It didn't offend me. His drug problem hadn't begun. You take a big flaming juicy ego like that and add drugs to it—it's no good. I mean, Freud thought he'd made great breakthroughs treating inferiority complexes with cocaine. Imagine what it does to add that to someone who's *already* Mr. Confidence!

I know he stretched me. I stretched him some too, inadvertently, on things like "Don Juan's Reckless Daughter." That was Alexandro Acuña, Don Alias, myself and Jaco. Alex's background is in Latin music, so that track was getting a very Latin percussion sound on the bottom. I said, "No, this is more North American Indian, a more limited palette of drum sounds." So Jaco got an idea. I don't know if he detuned his bass, but he started striking the end of the strings, up by the bridge, and he'd slide with the side of his palm all the way down to the head. He set up this pattern: *du du du doom, du du du doom.* Well, it's a five-minute song, and three minutes into it his hand started to bleed. He shredded it making it slide the full length of his bass strings. They turned into a grater. So we stopped taping and he changed to his Venus mound, below the thumb. And when we finished the take, that was bleeding, too. So his whole hand was bleeding. But the music was magnificent, and he was so excited because he'd discovered a new thing. Later he built up calluses and you'd always see him doing those slides. But then he was mad with me because I had copped his new shit for *my* record—and he wanted the new shit for *his* record! I think he might have had a different pain threshold.

Jaco was a self-proclaimed mutt. He had so many different bloodlines running through him. But one of them was Irish and I always felt that was fairly evident. Maybe it was an Irish spirit that the best of our communication went out on. Jaco, you know, was a *gerner*. A gerner is a funny-face maker. They have competitions in England. They pull their lips over their noses. A lot of the best gerners have no teeth— they can collapse their whole face. It's a folk art, and in rural places like the north of England, maybe Wales, they have contests where these hideous contortions are adjudicated. And Jaco was a master at it. He did all sorts of obscene things with his face. He'd say, "Do you want to see me make my face like a woman's pussy?" I swear! I don't know if I want to say this . . . but he'd do it. He'd turn his mouth so it went sideways, pull his lips into obscene shapes and I'd say, "Oh my God!" He was so much fun to be with.

He loved his kids; he was really good with kids and animals. Jaco was a great spirit before his deterioration by toxics. He'd come to L.A. to make his fortune, and spent a lot of time away from home. Once his wife called to say his child was mad with him because he never came home. Jaco said, "That's good, that's good, it shows the kid is thinking!" He had such a positive attitude about certain things. It was detached in a certain way, but not without warmth. I thought he had wonderful eyes before drugs clouded them. Look at that portrait of him on his first album cover and see if he doesn't look like some Tibetan sage.

He'd say, "I'm the baddest. I'm not braggin', I'm just telling the truth!" And I'd give him that. As far as I was concerned, he *was* telling the truth. It didn't even seem inappropriate to me that he knew it. But in order to keep the beauty of that bravado, you have to be able to back it up. And when his talent and inspiration began to be corroded by the clouding over of perception that accompanies overindulgence in drugs and alcohol, he became a tragic figure on the scene. Anyone who's that arrogant going up, people love to carve up going down. Therein lies the tragedy.

He started to get unruly, but I could deal with that. On *Don Juan's Reckless Daughter* there was a date where Henry Lewy and I waited for him. He was a hired hand coming in to play on a session, and he didn't show up. I thought I knew where we could find him. So when he was about two hours late I said, "Come on, Henry, we're going to go and get him." Sure enough, he and Wayne Shorter and Joe Zawinul and Peter Erskine, the drummer who had just joined Weather Report, were rehearsing for a tour. Wayne was up on the stage noodling around with the piano, and down on the floor were Jaco and Zawinul playing Frisbee. The two of them reminded me of European circus people: Zawinul and his straight back and shoulders like an Austrian tightrope walker, so proud, and Jaco had that same kind of command—he'd jump over the speakers; there were a lot of circus aspects to his performance. So here they were tossing this Frisbee around, Jaco catching it just like a circus act. "Ta-daa!" You could hear the trumpet fanfare. Then they threw it to Peter Erskine. Now, Peter was the new guy in the band. Boy, that thing was coming toward him and there was panic in his eyes. He caught it in kind of a wobbly way, and he wobbled it back to Zawinul. And they looked at him kind of like, "*Not the Flying Wallichi Brothers.*" They tossed it a few more rounds and then they tossed it to Wayne. Now, this was an insight into Wayne. Here was a Frisbee coming at him in his peripheral vision—he had both hands on the keyboards—and just at the perfect moment Wayne reached out his left hand, caught it and threw it back to them. He never turned his head, and he only took one hand off the keyboards.

When Jaco and I played one-on-one in the studio, it was a different thing. On *Mingus* there's a duet that we did, "God Must Be a Boogie Man." I heard that the other day and I thought, "God, I don't know how he hung in there with me!"

I let a long time go by between notes. I'd go *bomp* and he'd catch it with me! There'd be a lot of space. It wasn't like there was a band or somebody keeping metered time. I thought, "How did he do that?" Then I remembered, he used to watch my foot. My right foot would be keeping the steady time.

The *Shadows and Light* tour worked out fine, but it didn't look like it was going to. Jaco was musical director, and he didn't show up until we'd already been in rehearsal for about two weeks. When he did show up, he decided he didn't like the band. As we'd been rehearsing without a bass player, we'd kind of fleshed it in to where it sounded pretty good even without a bass. So when Jaco came, he started tearing the arrangements apart, demanding more space onstage. He later came to love everybody, but he didn't hear it that way initially. He didn't like Don Alias on drum kit, he liked him on hand drums. Well, I really liked the feel of Don's playing—he's not a technical virtuoso on the kit like he is on congas and other drums, where he's in the top three in the world, but he's such a good-*feeling* kit player to me. So we had this big argument and it didn't look like the thing was going to fly. As the tour rolled along, the tension dissolved—as a matter of fact, he took that band and played with them on his own record.

I think he played very well on that tour, especially, oddly enough, the day we filmed. Something personal had happened to him that day. I don't know what. Something between his wife and his mother, some family thing. He was in the midst of some tempering revelation. When we started, the first few notes he played were from "I Was High and Mighty." For a minute I thought, "I can't believe it! I'm watching Jaco have a humble attack! It's not really good for him to be this humble. Come on, Jaco, be a *little* arrogant!" Toward the end he took off, but he used to jump over his amp and beat his bass with his strap every night on that tour—this was the one night he didn't do it. It was a shame because Mike Brecker and I had cooked it up that when he jumped over the speakers and beat his bass, Mike was going to jump out and beat his saxophone. We were going to have a real donnybrook up there. I thought, "Maybe I'll come out and beat the piano." But he didn't do it.

There wasn't any real parting point between us; we stopped playing together because Jaco didn't play well anymore. Then I lost contact with him. It was more of a drifting apart than a breaking off. He went off with Weather Report and they played Japan and I heard tales of him jumping into fountains naked, going amok in the Orient. I just didn't see him that much.

I think he had a beautiful animal wisdom that I don't see as a *madness* at all. It's something that we lost. You could view it in this time as madness, and certainly it could be seen as a madness. Maybe I have the same madness but it's not so expressed. In Jaco I saw some of those expressions as a celebration of life. Strange behavior, certainly. But I love animals, and Jaco loved animals. To run down the street taking off his clothes was different if he did it from if you did it. I don't think of it as demented. I know he lost it at the end; you couldn't talk to him. It was tragic. And coke inflamed his mean side. Coke shuts off the heart and allows meanness or anything that's lying there—a cruel wit—to develop. We all have it. In whatever form, it's lying there.

I saw him for the last time in New York a couple of years ago. I went to an art opening with a group of people. We came out and were looking for a place to eat. We saw this little restaurant across the street with a hand-painted sign: JACO PASTORIUS TONIGHT. So I went across to see him. We all walked in and he was sitting at the bar. I went up and tapped him. When he turned his face to me he was just . . . gone. It was a gone face. He hugged me like he was drowning. Then he switched into this gear: he started yelling my name around the club. "Joni Mitchell is the baddest! She's the only woman this, she's the only woman that." Until it was embarrassing. Everyone there was embarrassed. The room was embarrassed, I was embarrassed. He kept hollering my name. It was a very small club, there were maybe ten people present. Anyway, we ended up jamming for a minute. I just got up and starting improvising on this electric piano. There was a vocal mike on it, with a cord draped along the back of the piano. At one point Jaco moved forward and he short-sheeted me for a joke; he pulled the cord down so it ran along the keyboard from the middle C down, an obstacle course. In trying to move it back up, I inevitably hit a clunker and somebody in the audience yelled out, "Never mind the mistakes, Joni." Jaco was laughing. So I just stopped and said, "Look, this isn't going to work. I'm just going to let Jaco play and I'll sing to him." So I grabbed the mike and let him take the lead. He'd used to play "out," but there's out and then there's *out*. This was not good. It was frustrating. It was heartbreaking. And so I just let him play and I followed him and sang with him. That way, no matter where he went I could try and be supportive. But he was not in the mood to be supportive. That particular evening, he was a saboteur.

The day after Jaco died I went back and listened to *Mingus*. I went back, basically, to reminisce. And gee, there was some beautiful communication in that playing. I hadn't listened to it for years. The grace of the improvisation on that record—there's space, and then one voice comes in. It's not three people grabbing, feeling a pressure point coming up and all landing on it at once. Jaco was not a road hog at that point. When you put him in that chemistry with Herbie and Wayne, I think they all played splendidly. "Courtesy" sounds so formal, but it was the best of musical manners. And the voices they speak in when they do come in! I thought that was some really good playing. And there were a lot of magic evenings like that.

—*December 1987*

SONNY ROLLINS:

THE CROSS AND THE ROSE

BY CHIP STERN

It's something fails us. First we feel. Then we fall.

JAMES JOYCE, *FINNEGANS WAKE*

YOU DON'T KNOW WHAT LOVE IS

The Manhattan workshop of Sonny Rollins—a tiny studio on the top floor of a Tribeca high-rise—seems to domicile an extremely studious NYU junior. To the left of his bed, a neat pyramid of books on Shintoism, Buddhism, Hinduism, Islam, Judaism, and Christianity is crowned by a portrait of an African drummer dancing against a brooding russet sky (the painter: The Prophet). Across the room to the right, shelves spill over with manu-

scripts, cassettes and one of those silly back-window-of-a-car bobbing-head dolls that hypnotize you in traffic snarls—only this one is of a beaming Satchmo. An Indian tamboura and a disheveled African gut-string instrument peer shyly from their respective corners; a punch-drunk piano creaks under the weight of manuscript paper; through an adjacent picture window, Manhattan's northern boulevards veer off frostily in eerie diagonal lines of night and light. Stretched out on the bed in jogging sweats and a floppy wool cap, Sonny Rollins's gentle eyes dominate the powerful axis point of his patrician nose.

> "A lot of guys say, 'I don't care about the people; I just play.' But I never met a musician who didn't want to reach people."

"I think my whole life has been a work in progress," Rollins is reflecting. "I've had a beautiful life, and I've played with some of the most fantastic musicians. And I was accepted by all the older guys as well as the beboppers. I remember playing at the Village Vanguard, and Roy Eldridge and Papa Jo Jones came to see me; and Jo was hollering, 'Yeah, Sonny! Sonny Rollins, all right . . .' and that made me feel so proud, you know, like they were giving me the nod. I always had the rhythm thing, the placement of notes. I was always gifted with the ability to swing.

"The part of Sonny Rollins that is unfinished," he goes on, "is that . . . well, I consider myself lucky that I've survived this far. A lot of cats withered away from all the pressures and pitfalls, but I changed my life around. It wasn't just about music when I got away from that scene for the first time [in 1959]. I quit to do a total reconstruction on every level of my life. I married Lucille; I began getting seriously into physical culture and weight lifting, which led me directly into the practice of yoga; I began reading a lot on metaphysics and philosophy. I turned around.

"Now when I look at myself there's more that I want to do, but I can see where somebody could isolate a period in the Fifties and say, 'Well, he had it together and it was a whole story.' I mean, I liked all of the good stuff. Like that trio album [*Live at the Village Vanguard*, Blue Note] with Wilbur Ware and Elvin [Jones]; I thought we had a nice free-swinging thing going. I liked *Way Out West* [Contemporary]—it was a nice idea and had some nice feeling on it. I dug *Freedom Suite* [Riverside], of course, because I had Max [Roach] and Oscar [Pettiford] on it, especially the concept of doing a whole piece of music as a suite—and the message of the music. I can appreciate all of that, but it's not relevant to the fact that I still think my stuff is unfinished—as a whole."

Therein lies the dilemma of *being* Sonny Rollins: No artist is more beloved by his audience, but then none inspires greater expectations than the saxophone colossus. At times Rollins must feel nearly cannibalized by this devotion. What's next? What's new? What have you done for me lately? Here is a musician, just shy of his nineteenth birthday, bouncing along with Fats Navarro and Bud Powell on that pianist's seminal 1949 Blue Note session. Accepted and encouraged by the tribal elders of improvisation, Rollins (Newk to his friends, owing to his striking resemblance to then–Brooklyn Dodgers pitching ace Don Newcombe) went on to become *the* icon of Fifties hard-bob tenor, much as his soul mate John Coltrane dominated the frenetic Sixties. Rollins's collaborations with Powell, Navarro, Benny Green, Thelonious Monk, Miles Davis, the Modern Jazz Quartet, J. J. Johnson, Clifford Brown, and

Max Roach, as well as his own trendsetting work as a leader, froze the embryonic image of the young improviser for three generations.

For so prodigious a talent, the recordings from that era are at once a blessing and a curse. For younger fans, great Rollins performances like "Oleo," "Pent-up House," "Pannonica," "Strode Road," "Old Devil Moon," "The Freedom Suite," and "Blessing in Disguise" have a life all their own. But for creative artists, recordings are also frozen time. Such moments shadow them wherever they try to grow, reminding listeners who were on *that* scene at *that* time, how much better things were. And nostalgia sets in.

Even if Sonny Rollins's Fifties recordings were only a ghost of what he was doing down live, I can sympathize with my elders. For beyond his extraordinary musicality— his mythic thematic intuition—there remains something surreal about that tone and groove; the bottomless brawn of the Rollins tenor, as notes blossom transparently in cubist shards and bulbous balloons of sound, the impudent grace of his swing, lines lazily coiling and uncoiling; improbable quotes and asides from his stream-of-consciousness; the deft way he builds anticipation with rhythmic and melodic motifs, then suddenly exceeds all expectations in a harmonic spillover of emotions and ideas that render his drummer, the song—even his tenor—totally irrelevant. Yeah—play it again, Sonny.

Still, unless you went off to Gettysburg with Eisenhower in 1961, it's worth noting that there have been some changes in music over the last thirty years, and in the way listeners perceive that music. Nowadays, kids of my daughter's generation don't really hear Tin Pan Alley melodies floating languidly above a set of moving changes in the treble clef—they hear melody coming out of the bass. The way songs are portrayed today is from the bottom up, out of the backbeat and the rhythms—all those rhythms. "Jazz" goes in one ear and out the other.

"Doesn't that bother you?" Sonny inquires earnestly. "Wouldn't that lack of communication be troubling? It concerns me—how do you connect with people when jazz as we understand it is not really in their environment? I mean, bebop never went away. It's still a foundation of musical knowledge.

"But," Sonny continued, "variety is an essential part of my presentation as well. I usually try and play a lot of styles. I hadn't wanted to play Fifties bebop in a long, long time—maybe since the Fifties. You know, when more rhythms came to the forefront and drummers began to play with more cross-rhythms; when different percussion instruments began to augment the rhythm section, and different sorts of grooves began to develop, that was very interesting to me. I've always loved rhythms as opposed to a band with piano, upright bass and a drummer going *ching-chinka-chink/chinka chink*—I just hear too many rhythms to be satisfied with that. I haven't maybe gotten my thing completely together yet, but I don't ever want the music to come across as one-dimensional."

This is a sore point with Sonny's older fans, for whom the past sixteen years have been a long, unsatisfying flirtation with the static rhythms of rock 'n' roll, redeemed only by the intermittent transmogrifications of the "real" Sonny Rollins in concert situations or live recordings like *Don't Stop the Carnival* (on Milestone). Without attempting to justify the moments of triviality that sometimes belabor his studio efforts, or explain his genial deference to sidemen who don't deserve to lick his ligature, I think it's superficial as hell to simply dismiss all of his studio work outright (dig *Horn Culture, Nucleus, Easy Living*, and *Don't Ask*)—because that misses the point. Which is that Sonny Rollins has always had an abiding affection for pop music in all forms.

During the sacred Fifties, Newk developed a reputation for transforming the most out-of-left-field pop songs and show tunes into joyous parodies or compelling personal statements, from "Toot, Toot, Tootsie" and "Rock-a-Bye Your Baby With a Dixie Melody" from the lexicon of Al Jolson, to the hard swing and boyish affection with which he showers "Wagon Wheels" and "I'm an Old Cowhand" from *Way Out West*. Or listen how, on 1966's *East Broadway Rundown*, his Latin airs and operatic bluesiness turn "We Kiss in the Shadows" (from *The King and I*) into the most sublime of jazz performances.

There you have the pop music of days long gone. So why should it be so surprising that Sonny Rollins is interested in the pop, dance, and R&B forms of today? His first great influence was Louis Jordan, a connecting link between the urban and rural blues traditions that evolved into swing, R&B, and rock 'n' roll; in conversation Rollins speaks admiringly about artists as diverse as Hank Williams, Robert Johnson, Frank Sinatra, Nat "King" Cole, Stevie Wonder, and James Brown. ("I always dug James Brown a lot. . . . I know that James Brown told a cat that he wanted to play with me one time.") Beneath him, you say? Hell, this is an artist who treats "Pop Goes the Weasel" to thematic variations worthy of Mozart at the opening of *The Solo Concert*.

True, what's been a work in progress for Sonny has been a prolonged slump to others. But this time, instead of going to the bridge or the ashram, Rollins went home to an upstate farm—sort of an elongated working sabbatical—where he alternately emerges and recedes with new ideas and refinements, pausing to reflect and recharge. Those forays and experiments in Sonny Rollins's music—good, bad and indifferent—are symbolic of a life's search, a process that must be viewed holistically.

Understand, that where some life cycles simply cease, others grind and grow powerful slow. The fact is, Rollins has been on a roll since his Rolling Stones guest shot on *Tattoo You* and his own production of *Sunny Days, Starry Nights* in 1984. Nor is the gusher of live, straight-no-chaser Sonny that fanatics found so exhilarating on *The Solo Album* and *G-Man* at all mitigated on his latest studio album, *Dancing in the Dark*, where Sonny and his band (trombonist Clifton Anderson, bass guitarist Jerome Harris, keyboardist Mark Soskin and drummer Marvin "Smitty" Smith) achieved the sort of collective chemistry, pacing and power we've come to expect from Newk in his best live shows. He's captured the loose spirit of a jazz band in the studio more effectively than at any point in the last sixteen years. Including that most beloved of his aspects— Sonny Rollins: The Spontaneous Orchestra.

Dancing's title tune is the tour de force of a balanced, engaging session. Newk's unaccompanied opening cadenza sets up a spider's web of complexity. He basks in the glow of Anderson's trombone, before ripping off an astonishing series of variations, trampling bar lines and chord changes in his wake without negating his gruff, operatic lyricism. More to the point, Sonny Rollins sounds as if he's having a good time—he's not holding anything back, and that is unprecedented in his studio efforts since *Next Album*. Like so much of his work from the past sixteen years, he doesn't achieve his effect simply through harmonic means, but through colorful manipulations of timbre and pitch. It's as if Sonny has been chipping away at the edge of his dark round sound over the years, revealing layers of color and a percussive edge. It is a very, well, grandfatherly kind of sound, that puts this writer in mind of the grandfather of the tenor, Mr. Coleman Hawkins. Additionally, "O.T.Y.O.G" chases the train at a brisk gallop, and "Allison" frames the lyrical side of Rollins's writing and improvising in a charming medium-up stroll that suggests Tadd Dameron to some well-traveled ears. So maybe entrenched jazzbos and critic types will finally find something to like in *Dancing in the Dark*.

"Well," Sonny says, "I try not to worry about the critics anymore. They can dislike you or like you depending on what the consensus is. I guess they get together and form an opinion. Is that what you guys do?" he asks mischievously.

"It's a no-win situation," I reply. "Because you command the greatest love, you create the greatest expectations. We're always wondering how come the Sonny Rollins we love and the Sonny Rollins you love are invariably so disparate. Like, I dig a lot of what you've done on records recently, but number one on my wish list . . . do you know what that is?"

"What."

"Trio," I say prayerfully.

"Oh, really," he replies quizzically. "Well, that's nice, but you know that I think that is very avant-garde. Maybe people would accept that—I don't know."

"Well," I press on insistently, "is it a question of people accepting it or you accepting it?"

"As far as my accepting it, it takes very good players— very strong bassists and drummers. Anytime I had a combination where I could have done that, I already had a band—there were other guys involved. But I'm certainly not averse to the idea of playing with a trio again; in other words, that's a hint, right?" He smiles, then goes on to consider maybe doing it as part of a set, when the phone rings and he's saved by the bell.

"Anyway," I go on as he hangs up the phone, "no writers could possibly be harder critics on Sonny Rollins than Sonny Rollins."

"That's true," he agrees, "I'm a very tough critic of myself."

"When *G-Man* came out I was beside myself. Wow, they finally captured Sonny going berserk in a live situation. The way you twisted the harmony inside out, those incredible long-held tones, the multiphonics, that one high note at the beginning that sounds like an enraged Electrolux, just the unbelievable intensity of it. I thought, 'Gee, this is historic, this is a breakthrough, I want to go out in the street and yell hooray and walk through ground glass and hot coals in my bare feet.' Then when I came down I figured, 'Well, Sonny probably hates it,' right?"

Newk explodes in loud laughter. "Well, okay, that is true," he admits. "I'm glad people liked it, but I didn't do what I wanted to do; plus I got a horn that I'd just gotten fixed, which meant that it was different than usual—it takes a while to break a horn in. So I was very frustrated on that; it was not what I wanted to do at all."

"My horn-player friends are always fidgeting to get the reeds and ligature and action together—horns are funny."

Newk chuckles. "Ha ha ha. Yeah. horns are funny—that's a good title for a tune," he says, then becomes distant. "No, you never get that stuff right. Making art is something that you never . . ." and his voice fades into an ellipse of thought, still trying to get it right—better, even better.

"You know," he continues, "I do care what people think about me; and I care what the so-called critics think, of course. It's a no-win situation because . . . how can you ever live up to everything a person might want you to be? There are things on some albums that I like, but I think there's a facet of me playing that hasn't been recorded yet. I definitely feel that way. So I'm not about to look back and say this was good and that was good. I'm still in the race actually, and there's still things I want to work on. So I just try and keep my own sights straight. But it certainly is a great feeling to know that you are loved and/or hated for your work."

"Oh, God, nobody hates you, Newk," I insist. "Why do you suppose that all of us were hollering for you to do a solo album all these years? Because we wanted to kill your bands; get rid of these chumps so that we can listen to Sonny."

"Right," he laughs, "instead of shoot the piano player, shoot the whole band. I am wont to play a lot of solos and take long cadenzas and so forth. Actually, I'm trying to express myself completely; present the Sonny Rollins everybody is expecting to hear, you know. The bands are there because it's a convention—you want to hear a band playing, have a good-sounding group. I might be able to play solo for the rest of my life, but that would be pretty energy-consuming—I don't know if I could handle that.

"I'm trying to reach a collective type of improvisational thing with the group—the basic spirit of jazz. I'm a jazz player and I want the band to sound like a real good jazz band. There was a period in my life when I used to fire piano players, so I have had periods when I couldn't get people to follow me, and I guess I was a little more volatile at that point. But everybody isn't the same. The very fact that I have a group of people accompanying me would tend to suggest that they are accompanists rather than leaders. But that's also an art, to follow people—and to follow me you have to have certain skills."

"Do you favor accompanists over collectivists?" I wonder.

"I've tried both," he replies. "I've tried a lot of different combinations during my life as a bandleader.... I don't know.... I'm not sure. I think as a bandleader you want to have people you can mold in a way that they get out the music that I want to portray. So I'm not looking for guys who have to express themselves *all* the time. I think that playing with me, the guys who are quote-unquote "accompanists" have a lot of room to express their emotions and feelings and get out their own music. Playing with me I think is very easy, because they have a lot of space to express themselves within the context of the compositions. I don't tell them how to solo or what to play. I don't like to tell anybody anything; they should sort of know. So when I say mold, I mean I want to mold a group to present my picture: the picture I have in my mind of the sound I'm trying to project.

"Let me tell you something. There's a lot of guys who say, 'I don't care about the people—I just play.' But I have never met a musician who didn't want to reach the people. You don't dance onstage unless you feel like dancing; you don't do things that are completely repugnant to yourself. Now you're playing for yourself first, of course, but then you want to reach somebody. Because, well, you may be great but how do you know if nobody likes you? Maybe I'm a little sensitive about people thinking I'm playing music to reach people—I'm playing to reach myself.

"We're just instrumental musicians, and if I could sing like Louis Armstrong I would probably try to—the human voice is the first instrument, and that's really the greatest instrument if you can use it. You see, when you get up on that stand, it is a show, whether you're consciously entertaining or not. The curtain rises, the lights are out. But instrumental musicians don't have many tools—all we can do is use music. To me there is no real connection with entertainment as it's known in singing groups and dancing groups. So yes, I do want to communicate with people, but no, I'm not an entertainer. I still want them to have a positive experience, but not at the expense of music. I want them to think, also, and I want them to feel more optimistic when they a leave a Sonny Rollins performance than when they came in—feel a little happier if that's possible in this fucked-up world."

And they do, but then they're only listening to Sonny Rollins, and when Saint Newk has packed up his horn and headed north again, the challenge remains—to *be* Sonny Rollins. To try and clear the vessel, to fine-tune it, to test it so that he can be a channel for his own emotions and longings and fantasies; more importantly, so that he can truly be the *new man*, be a channel for things older and stronger and more eternal than Sonny Rollins; so that all of this can come through him—in a pure gush of love and freedom sweet, oh so sweet.

Rollins looks out the window into the gusty winter night, and there's that faraway look in his eyes again, as we talk of things that guide us through time on our way to spaces unknown. There is death in the air, but it does not beckon as a threat, rather as a promise, a hint of something beyond us yet beside us all the while—a life's work just to prepare and move on. A Mozart, a Robert Johnson, a Jimmy Blanton, Charlie Christian, Clifford Brown; a Charlie Parker, a Hendrix. Walking among us for but an instant, no more, giving us a glimpse of something unimaginably beautiful, then having the bad luck or good sense to swoop the sphere before someone can ask them ... *what's next*? Suddenly, what little they may have left behind is precious beyond compare; treasured, pored over and dissected and analyzed and worshiped until some begin to sense its meaning—its truth. No next album, just the living residue of legend and myth to guide us and beckon. And what of those left behind, the survivors, the disciples? What is left to discover, to reveal?

Sonny Rollins grows quiet. He's still dancing in the dark

after all these years. "Chip," he asks softly, "what do you suppose Coltrane would be playing now?"

THE SOLO CONCERT
MORPHEUS

Who's to say what is real? I've had some real dreams in my life. I had a dream when my mother died; we weren't getting along at the time, and then she died suddenly. And after a while she came back to me in a dream, and I know it was real—a religious experience. I haven't dreamed about Coltrane in years and years, but I had a dream about him the other night—maybe because I was talking to you about him. It wasn't just a vision, it was very realistic. We were hanging out together, like back in the old days. We were talking, and he was telling me some of his stories with his wry sense of humor. It was very upbeat; everything was harmony and love, you know, and when I woke up I was happy—smiling. I'm sure glad he came back.

WEST END BLUES

When I think of the spiritual, I think of Louis Armstrong. I read where Django Reinhardt said that the first time he heard Louis Armstrong, he cried. Very spiritual. Very much beyond the physical, it's definitely beyond that—joy!

I remember with Miles, when we'd be breaking between sets, and Louis Armstrong would be up the street and Miles'd say, "Hey, let's go dig Pops." For me it was not so much hearing Louis Armstrong, although of course I used to listen to him—that '27–'28 music is some real bad stuff—but when I used to see Louis Armstrong, that did a lot for me. . . . just like a picture I had in a book one time when I was in India . . . and this guy who knew nothing about jazz—he saw this picture of Charlie Parker, and he got something from the picture, you know what I mean? He could feel Bird's strength. So seeing Louis Armstrong, that gave me a feeling, made me feel uplifted. The music is great; man, Louis Armstrong did everything but just being in his physical presence, you could feel the music and depth of his musical personality. I love him.

DUKE OF IRON

When I was young, I mean really young, I did a lot of sketching and watercolors. I can paint; I just haven't gotten back into it since I've been in music—I'd like to, though, if I can find the time. I was always sketching. Someone told me that Wayne Shorter used to do comic books when he was a kid. I used to too. I was into heroes: the original Blue Beetle, the Human Torch and Toro, Captain America and Bucky, the Submariner. The Submariner was nasty, man; he could stay underwater and fly with these little wings on his ankles. I dug Captain America, and that cat who created him . . . Jack Kirby—he was my man! I couldn't draw hands; I never could draw hands, so I'd have to have the guy holding something.

I sort of remember trying to get this character called the Chain. He was a strong guy, and the biceps were bulging, and chains were breaking up all over him; I think I conceived of him having certain powers. I remember the Chain especially because I'd gotten a whole book together with the boxes and all; I'd written most of it out and gotten all of it drawn, and I put some staples in it, which was a big thing in those days—put some staples in it and it was just like a magazine. He was all ready to go. I reached my peak with the Chain, I think.

See, there were guys who were good and guys who were bad. So I prided myself on this kind of attitude, you know, like sticking up for poor people that couldn't take care of themselves against guys who would take advantage of them—I bought the whole thing. This is still the case. In fact, when we lived in Brooklyn, I used to go out at night and sort of patrol the area; I had two big shepherds, and I thought of myself as being there to fight crime if we encountered anything on the streets.

HARLEM BOYS

It was just great to grow up in Harlem. I was born between Lenox and Seventh Avenues on 137th Street. Then we moved up economically, and my family moved from downtown Harlem to Sugar Hill . . . around 1939, when I was nine. 150th and Edgecombe, up by the Polo Grounds. I used to see Carl Hubbell and his funny left arm. At that time blacks were living up as far as maybe 165th Street; then you got to the Heights and there were certain streets you didn't venture beyond. There was a gang up there called the Rainbows, a bad Irish gang.

Above 145th Street, you were up on Sugar Hill, where the nicer brownstones and apartments were. All the top black musicians lived up on the hill, because that was the only good place they could live; *all* the cats—it was some neighborhood. Duke Ellington, Erskine Hawkins, Coleman Hawkins, Don Redman, Jimmy Lunceford, Sid Catlett and John Kirby—oh, man. Mary Lou Williams had an apartment up on Hamilton Terrace; I think it's a landmark site now. I grew up with people like Jackie McLean, Art Taylor and Kenny Drew, among those who made it to the big time. That whole area was great—it was the center of the Harlem cultural community.

At that time, most of the cats you'd want to see play, you had to come up to Harlem. Later there were clubs downtown on 52nd Street, like the Hurricane Club, where

Duke Ellington used to play, once black musicians were able to go downtown to play—to me, that was the beginning of the end of Harlem. And drugs, of course. As soon as black people were able to live in different places, they dispersed, and there went the energy that was Harlem.

SCHOOL DAYS (WHEN WE WERE KIDS)

My father was in the navy, so he was away when I was born, and I was conscious of meeting him. I must have been two or three. When I was small there was a xylophone I used to play around on. I was the baby of the family, and both my older brother and sister were excellent musicians and went on to attend the Music and Art High School in New York; Music and Art was a hell of a hard high school to get into in those days. My brother played a lot of violin, and piano, too; my sister played piano, and also majored in art—so we're all talented in those ways. I remember laying in bed and hearing my brother practicing; I really liked the sound of that violin. My dad said he played clarinet at one time, but I never saw it . . . and my mother was just a very special person.

I had an uncle who took me by his girlfriend's apartment, and she had all these records by guys like Lonnie Johnson, Big Boy Crudup and Tommy McClennan—these were *real* blues cats, man. Sometimes they'd leave me there, and I'd listen to all these records. She also had some Louis Jordan, who was like a bridge between the blues and jazz—he had a great big sound on the alto, and I just loved him. Later on, Louis Jordan and the Tympany Five got more showbizzy, and I followed everything they did really closely. They would be on all the jukeboxes in Harlem, and used to play at a club—the Elks Rendezvous—right across the street from my elementary school P.S. 89. They would have Louis Jordan's picture outside—one of those eight-by-tens. He had this great-looking horn, shiny like a samurai's sword, and these sharp ties and tails the cats used to wear. I said, "*Man*, this is it for me—I've got to go this way."

TENOR MADNESS

Somewhere in that period after Louis Jordan I began to be more aware of big band music and radio jazz. I began to go to the Apollo Theatre and hear radio broadcasts from there; Benny Carter and Nat "King" Cole used to do shows together. Somewhere in there, I don't remember where, I began to hear Coleman Hawkins—maybe it was "Body and Soul." To me, he was a cat who played involved and sophisticated conceptions as distinct from Louis Jordan, who was more earthy and blues oriented. I really dug the change as something deeper . . . well, I don't want to say that, but perhaps more difficult to get to; it would require a more serious attempt at playing.

I knew Coleman because he lived right around the corner from me; I used to see him a lot. He was always very well dressed, and he carried himself in a very sophisticated way; a very taciturn man, but that was sort of a mask. For me he was a role model, besides being a musical idol. I remember waiting for him outside his house one day with my eight-by-ten glossy of Coleman Hawkins, you know; and I waited and waited and waited; and finally he came and I said, "Oh, Mr. Hawkins, would you sign this for me?" I've still got that picture.

Your tone always reminded me of Hawk, but the spaciousness of your line always suggested Prez. It's almost like subtractive improvising, where you airbrush away the extraneous notes, just to get to the meat of the melody—the core of the idea.

*   *   *

It's very interesting that you should say that. I heard Coleman Hawkins one night, playing one of the last gigs he did before he died, and he was not well; he was not playing with all of the notes he usually used—maybe he was having trouble breathing. But his playing that night had a profound effect on me. Because in a way he had peeled away all these other notes, and it was fantastic. He was just playing the *essential notes.*

Lester was like that—Lester was something else. He used to room with some people we knew up on Hamilton Terrace, so I used to see him frequently, walking around with his porkpie hat on, the whole silhouette and everything, and we'd whisper, "Look, there's Lester Young, man." And he was very cool and all by himself in a world all his own.

I liked him when he came out of the army, when he was playing songs like "Up'n Adam." The late-Fifties approach Lester had was real light and airy, real relaxed—he was so expressive. I dug that. And guys said, "Well, you should have heard him when he was out popping in front of the Basie band, that was the greatest!" But to me, he had gotten more introspective later and was really speaking more.

MISTERIOSO

I got with Monk when my friend Lowell Lewis—a very fine trumpeter—got with the band. We were still in school, and after classes we'd go for rehearsals down at Monk's apartment. Somehow he worked it out so they finagled this other tenor player out of the band, and Monk hired me.

He was the type of guy who would never tell you what to play; if he liked you, here was the music, and that's that. A lot of his music was challenging, to say the least. I remember these trumpet players telling him, "Man, you

220

can't play this stuff; you can't make jumps like this." But eventually we would end up playing this unorthodox and hitherto unplayed material.

I looked up to him as a father figure—a guru, really, he was really into that music—that's all Monk cared about. One time he told me, "Man, if there wasn't music in this world, this world wouldn't be shit."

UN POCO LOCO

Bud Powell was known in the neighborhood as a sort of mad-genius type. So it was really great in 1949 when he was making this record for Blue Note and he said, "Yeah, I want you." I remember on one of those dates I made a mistake on the music and Bud looked over at me.... I mean, he really gave me a look. That was the last time I made that mistake. Though I don't know how I got it to-gether after that look he shot me. He was very high-strung, man.

Bud used to take me around and we'd hang out. In my observing Bud, it seemed as if he was putting people on a lot, which is not to say that he didn't have real breakdowns at times or that being in and out of those hospitals didn't weaken him a lot. But it was also a way to keep people off him—like, "Boy, this cat is weird."

I felt very close to Bud, and Monk did, too, of course, and we'd go to visit him in the mental hospitals, several times. We used to go way the hell out to Central Islip, all the way out on Long Island, and one time were in there ... you've got to picture this. All the cats used to dress in street clothes; there were no uniforms or hospital outfits. And we went in to see Bud, trying to talk to him: "Well, how do you feel, man, how are you doing?" Suddenly I saw this guy closing the doors, and I said, "Whoa, man! We're just vis-iting."

OLEO

Miles is Miles. You can't destroy that kind of musician. He can't destroy himself. He's just there—always.

BEWARE, BROTHER, BEWARE/PARADOX

I didn't have the average childhood. I didn't get a chance to go to schools where they really emphasized sports or scholastics. I feel very bad about this, because I know I have a good mind, and if I had been taken in tow by counselors and teachers, I think I could have had a different life in many ways. They gave you a smattering of academics—enough that it wouldn't do you any good—and kept you off the streets for a few years. Most of the guys didn't finish it, but I felt I had to. Still, I was involved with nothing in my school at all. I didn't even play with the band.

And we had to fight to get to school; they had all these race riots and stuff, you know, like "Oh, they're trying to send the blacks down in our neighborhood." We had fights every day with the Italian boys, and the neighbors in the houses would throw stuff out the windows as we were walking back across town—the same old shit.

I graduated from high school in 1948. Heroin was just getting out into the neighborhoods; it was cheap and it was plentiful. That's when I got hooked.

You see, Billie Holiday was using. And Charlie Parker. Those were really two powerful artists, and when we found out that Billie Holiday used drugs, and Charlie Parker used drugs, we figured it can't be all that bad—and maybe that's the key to creativity. Charlie Parker was a dream. He was such a leader for us, he did so much. We saw him as a Jesus Christ figure who got crucified for standing up for freedom, and even the fact that he used drugs—that was a sacrament of sorts.

The drugs were just a way to get into the music more, I believe—to shut out everything but the music. It wasn't just about getting off on a side trip; it was let's go, we'll get high, and we'll play—because that's all we did. It was about getting high and playing.

What finally made you decide to quit?

I didn't finally decide to quit—I had to quit, man. Because I had messed up that bad. I was over on Riker's Island—the Rock. I was in there twice, came out once, got hooked again, and went back in the joint for a parole violation. Came out and got hooked again. I was in bad shape. I had stolen from my best friends—I didn't have any friends. I had taken everything from my house. An old friend told me recently when he was coming to New York, Max Roach told him one thing: "Stay away from Charlie Parker, and stay away from Sonny Rollins." I didn't realize I was that bad at the time. But I was living like an animal, sleeping in parked cars, sleeping on the street, riding the subways all night long. I had no place to go.

Now I had some incentives. My mother stood by me all the way. She was really the only one—because I had burned everybody. I'll tell you one very scary thing that happened to me, which sort of brought it all home—one of the things that makes me believe in God, because you're talking about having to pray. Bud Powell came out of the hospital; he had been in for a period of time. And I met Bud, and he said, "Hey man, how are you doing—let's get high." So . . . okay . . . we went, and I copped and everything, because he'd just got back and didn't know where to go. So we went up onto the top floor of some building around the 140s off of Seventh Avenue, and Bud took his stuff and passed out. And then it hit me—suppose Bud dies.

Then I would in effect have killed him. I didn't shoot him up, but I bought the drugs, and we were together—we were together. And I said, "Please, God, don't let this happen." Then the seriousness of what we were doing struck home a little bit, and fortunately he came out of it. He'd been away for a long time, and his system was really clean, and it just knocked him out, but it could have killed him, too. Guys were dying of overdoses—that was nothing strange. And I realized: This is the last I'm going to do something stupid like that.

So that, and my mom, and this incident with Charlie Parker sort of brought me around. It was the time of that record date of Miles's, you know, with "Compulsion," where he had Bird and me on tenors. And Bird at that time was not a happy man. He was getting into all sorts of stupid things, like getting put out of Birdland, if you could imagine something as ridiculous as that. And I guess he was needing money, and was in pretty bad shape during that entire period. And I perceived that one of his biggest problems was that all of these kids were getting high because of him, and there was nothing he could do about it—because he was hooked himself and couldn't stop, and all his disciples were using. That was one of the biggest hurts of his life. So he asked me, "Well, Sonny, how are you doing? Are you cool?" And I said, "Yeah, man I'm straight, now." So later on, Philly Joe told him, "Yeah, Sonny was over there getting high." And Bird's whole attitude toward me changed; he never spoke to me again. So that was something. Then I went and said, "Well, I'm going to show Bird that I can be cool." That was a big incentive for me to stop. And that's when I ended up in Lexington. I wanted to straighten out for Bird and for my mother, because she was my last friend—but Bird died before I could show that I'd really gotten his message. . . .

I met Clifford Brown when he was on this record date—I think it was Lou Donaldson's session—and Elmo Hope was the pianist. Elmo and I had collaborated on a tune ("Carvin' the Rock") which they were going to record. So I went by the session and that's when I think I first met Clifford. I didn't really see him when he was playing with Art Blakey and all those guys at Birdland—I must have been off the scene at the time. And I never ran into him in Philly. So I really met Clifford when Roach and Brown Incorporated passed through Chicago in 1955. The band was just starting to get known at that time, and they were working around the country; maybe they weren't working that much, because gigs weren't that plentiful during that period. So Harold Land's wife was pregnant, and she wanted him to come home, so he left the band, and they were looking for someone else. Of course I knew Max and Richie Powell, and that's when I went by and got in the band. I felt I evolved musically, emotionally and personally in that period because Brownie was such a wonderful person on every level; he had a profound influence on me as a man—here was a guy who was really a channel for all of this fantastic music, without getting hung up on any side trips. We were both the same age. He was a very pixieish-looking guy; and his humility was something, because here's a guy who just did it every night—every night on the trumpet, man. *On the trumpet.* Brownie's chops were there every night—phenomenal. In retrospect, he was one of these guys who was just too nice to really stay alive—too good to be in this world. . . . I'm telling you, when Brownie and Richie died, George [Morrow] and Max and me just bawled like babies. It was too much. He was a beautiful musician, and to this day, guys are still sounding a lot like him: Wynton sounds a lot like Brownie in a way; and Freddie; and Woody—all the guys in fact.

And Booker Little.

Booker Little. . .mmmmm. He was a beautiful kid, man. I call him a kid because he was a kid when I met him. A beautiful young cat. At that time when I was in Chicago in 1955, I had a day job as a porter and I was living at the Y, getting by on whole-wheat bread and tomato juice. I had a goal, which was to stay away from drugs and get myself together for the music. So Booker used to come by the Y, and we'd practice together in the basement, he couldn't have been more than sixteen or seventeen years old—isn't that something? And he was really playing, man. He was like one of these people who just visit the earth, and when I found out he had uremia, when Max told me he just had a certain amount of time to live, I just thought my God—I couldn't believe it. Because he was such a young vital cat, and sure enough, he was gone after only making a couple of records. It was a wonderful experience to know people like Booker and Clifford in this lifetime—they were like angels.

Like Eric Dolphy.

Eric! Man . . . Eric was beautiful. I was so mad at Miles; the week that Eric died, there was this Blindfold Test in *Down Beat* where Miles was talking about how bad Eric sounded and how he would step on his shoes and all that. And you see, Miles can get away with all this kind of stuff because he's cute and he's a dandy, but you know . . . Miles talks too much about people, and whether it's true or not, fuck it—don't say it. Anyway, I'll accept Miles if he wants to be like that; I mean, I'll accept whatever he wants to say about me or anybody, but that time it really came back on him—I know he must have had some feelings about it.

Every horn gives you a different sound, really, and every mouthpiece gives you a different sound, and the reeds give you a different sound. In my case, they give you a new perspective. If I play a new horn, it gives me a whole new palette. It's as if I decided to play a euphonium or something, just a completely different instrument, except it's one I know and can deal with.

There are some horn players, like Illinois Jacquet, who play one horn and that's it. I'm the type of guy who likes to change every few years or so—it's like getting a new lease on life. But I still keep most of my old horns, because I never know when I'd like to go back. A lot of it has to do with the physical mechanisms, the way they react to your constant pounding. But I play so hard and I practice so long that I get to the point where I kind of wear out a horn. . . . That's not exactly the right way to say it. You kind of get used to it and it's not giving you back enough.

Horns are very mysterious. There are certain parts of the room where the horn just projects better, where the sound is more friendly, you know. That's why I walk around the stage a lot—I'm trying to find that sweet spot. That's very important. There are some parts of a given stage you can't use; but there are some spots you try and find where the horn speaks back to you—and you hear what they're hearing.

I think they've tried and tested all sorts of metals for saxophones, and they found that, for overall resonance and sound, brass is best. So now that's what I'm using—a straight brass Selmer tenor. I've tried everything else, too. Silver horns tend to be a little brighter to my ears, and the quality is a little more brittle and the sound more difficult to control. Their tone is not quite as centered. The gold horn has what a lot of people refer to as a dark sound. Maybe more mellow or more focused might better describe the gold horn. The metal isn't always the determining factor—the shape of the horn is critical. For instance, I have one beautiful old gold Selmer Mark VI, and it has a gorgeous sound, but unfortunately the horn has never played completely in tune.

Lester Young played a silver Conn, but Lester Young was the exception in just about everything; and Chu Berry played a Conn. All of the guys played Conn early on. Even Charlie Parker made a lot of his breakthroughs on a Conn. Later on he went to a King. Alto players like Johnny Hodges used to play a Buescher. Bueschers are beautiful horns. As a matter of fact I went to a Buescher in the mid-Sixties. I was overseas, and I had a Selmer, and I got the notion to take the horn apart one day, and I had a concert that night. So I ended up borrowing a Buescher from this guy in Holland, and I just loved it; later the poor fella died, and I went back and bought the horn from his wife. I think I played that horn on "Alfie's Theme."

I thought the most beautiful sound Bird got was on that cheesy plastic alto at Massey Hall.

That's the way I felt when I played that guy's Buescher in Europe. It played so easy, and it sang, and it was just so easy to play compared to a Selmer, which is a little harder to hear. You see, the virtue of a Selmer is that right up close you might not be able to hear it, but in the back of the house you can hear it—that's the difference. Like I think the Yamaha tenor has it all except the metal, in my opinion. They are very good horns, and I endorse the Yamaha soprano, but on tenor it's hard to get away from the Selmer. It has more guts; and that's where you get the real tenor sound. You can put more energy into it and it'll take more without going out of tune and losing its pitch—so you can simply ignore the horn and let the music come through you. I don't even want to know I have a horn there—I want the music to play itself.

THE CUTTING EDGE

I'm not the kind of guy who puts himself up as being the greatest this or that, and I hate to say this—because I don't want it to sound like back patting or whining—but there are so many things I came across over the years that I wanted to develop on the tenor that I had to sort of curtail because of dental problems and operations I've had over the years. I've just barely scratched the surface.

It's just a matter of what you want to do. Who would have thought years ago that guys would be playing wind instruments using all these circular breathing things, holding a tone indefinitely? There's all kinds of expressions that haven't been developed. With different mouthpieces, I've gotten enough notes that it sounds like chords; where you can play a note lower than the lowest note on the tenor, and not by slipping your hand over the bell either.

And guys say, "Oh Sonny, that's impossible." But I don't think there's anything that can't be done. Because music is such a spiritual thing, man.

There's a place where I believe you can transcend these metal instruments and go to another area where you can impose a spiritual reality on the music you are playing. If you have the determination, if you have the faith, if you have the ear of God, you can do any of these things.

—May 1988

CAN'T STOP WORRYING,

CAN'T STOP GROWING:

TONY WILLIAMS

REINVENTS HIMSELF

BY TONY
SCHERMAN

■

This may sound self-aggrandizing, but playing the drums was always easy for me. From an early age, it was so easy to figure stuff out it was almost embarrassing. I needed to prove to myself that I was deserving of all the praise, needed to feel that I'd accomplished something—that I had accomplished something, the person that I am. I needed to tackle something that was hard, that wasn't God-given, and see it grow. That's what writing music has been, and is, for me. I had to go get a teacher, I had to study composition for seven years. That was work. Writing music, that's work. Drumming has never been work, it's always been fun. It's still fun. So I could never put the word 'work' in my life, and how can you be a success to yourself if you've never had to work?"

As he enters middle age, Tony Williams looks less and less African American, more and more exotic, near-Eastern: Persian, Lebanese, Assyrian. In profile, his nose hooks luxuriantly. His big almond-shaped eyes are sleepy and liquid; their blank stare can be unnerving. He wears his hair semi-straightened now, brushed back into a stiff little ducktail, and with his lazy rolling gait and odd-shaped body—thick biceps, thick waist—he looks like an ill-tempered Buddha.

Tony Williams—a handful. He plays like the rushing wind, like an avalanche, like a natural disaster. People look at each other and start to laugh, he's so good, so *loud*, so unapologetically in their faces. There's nothing polite about Tony Williams's drumming, nor anything overly diplomatic about him. He's testy, suspicious, self-involved. Still, the gibe I've heard more than once—"the only thing bigger than Tony Williams's talent is his ego"—strikes me as untrue. Beneath the cold manner flickers a real vulnerability: unhealed wounds. I'll bet he's easily devastated. Something gnaws at this guy, some basic insecurity, and if it makes him difficult and defensive, it's also made him hungry to learn. How many drummers can write a fugue? Compose for string quartet? Organize a spectacularly tight five-man jazz group and write every bit of its thirty-song repertoire—sinuous, muscular, haunting pieces? Williams's composing hasn't yet approached the level of his playing (how many drummers could you non-fatuously call "the world's greatest"?), but his achievement is pretty amazing: He's willed a new facet of himself into being.

Back in 1963, Tony was already working hard, if somewhat in the dark, at composing. "When I was a kid I thought this was what you did: you worked at whatever there was to get better at. Being a good musician meant to keep studying, keep learning. You didn't just specialize. Even back then, the thing that drove me on was wanting to do more, to have a say, to create an atmosphere."

Herbie Hancock, a former prodigy himself, was a suave twenty-three to the kid's eager-beaver seventeen. "Tony was always calling me up: 'Hey man! What's happening!' and I'd think, 'Aw kid, don't bothah me!' and try to gracefully get him off the phone." Callow or not, the kid was an astonishing drummer. When the pair joined the Miles Davis Quintet that spring, says Hancock, "I very quickly went from thinking of Tony as someone who was a real good drummer for a kid to realizing he was a great drummer who happened to be a kid." Thirty years later, Hancock is still an intrigued Williams-watcher. "Tony Williams," he says, "is one of the most intelligent people I have ever known."

When Tony wrote the songs for his first album, 1964's *Life Time*, he played piano with two fingers, "one on his right hand," says Hancock, "one on his left. No chords really, just two lines, and I had to write out the notes for him. His writing was very raw. But I wasn't about to dismiss something because it was a two-fingered composition; knowing the kind of mind Tony had, I just wanted to not get in his way, to help him realize whatever he had in the back of his head. And I still think the compositions on those first two albums [*Life Time* and *Spring*] were great.

"Today he's mastered the vocabulary, but without losing the beauty of that rawness. He's got a full palette now, from angular and surprising to very singable, very beautiful in the conventional sense. My feeling is, he has really got the compositional approach down. Tony doesn't need to study with anybody, at least not for a long while! I'll put it this way. Wayne Shorter and Stravinsky are my favorite composers of all time. Tony is developing so quickly as a composer that he's already one of my favorite jazz composers, and maybe moving toward being one of my favorite composers, period. I absolutely like his pieces that much."

Miles liked them, too; the Davis Quintet's classic Sixties albums are sprinkling Williams tunes like "Pee Wee" and "Hand Jive." But for Tony, "writing always felt hit-and-miss: 'Maybe this'll work, maybe it won't, why won't it?' " He had taken sporadic private lessons in theory and harmony since the mid-Sixties; 1979, however, was a turning point. He'd left Manhattan for the San Francisco Bay Area (where he still lives) "feeling in a hole, in a rut; I felt like I wasn't doing what I had the talent to do: write music, have a band, have better relationships." He thought about quitting music. Instead, he started private lessons in composition, mostly with Robert Greenberg, a young composer and university professor.

"It was a regular course of study, like at a university. You do a lot of analyzing of other people's work: Mozart, Beethoven, Brahms. I started with species counterpoint, went to intermediate forms of counterpoint, like canons, then invertible counterpoint, like fugues, and on to larger forms of composition—minuet and trio, theme and variations, rondo, that type of thing. It's all about learning how to weave structure and melody into a composition." When a recharged Williams launched his quintet in 1986, some of the band's best pieces came straight from his exercise book—"Arboretum" was an assignment in counterpoint, "Clear Ways" in voice-leading. Tony left Greenberg three years ago; "the band started working so much, I couldn't do my lessons. But I plan to go back and pick up where I stopped."

Before 1979, Williams says, "I knew everything there is to know about harmony and theory. What I mean is, I had a good solid grounding in all that stuff. But I didn't know how to organize. You might know emotionally what you want to say, but then it becomes a matter of getting the material to move where you want it to. It's problem-solving. For me it was like, 'I know there's a problem here but I don't know what it is.' When I come up to a problem now, I can pinpoint it. On *paper*. I can look at it and say, 'Oh, that's the problem and it's because of this, this and this, so if I adjust this, take that out, move this in' . . . problem solved."

What kind of problem, how to resolve a chord? "No, not how to resolve a chord, that's easy. How to expand an idea. How to make it go somewhere and then return. My big problem used to be that I agonized over things. I'd get an idea and not know what to do with it. Now when I get an idea, I know what to do. Writing is just being able to, as Bob Greenberg used to say, push notes around. Make the notes do what you *want* them to do.

"Sometimes when I was studying I'd wonder, 'What the hell am I doing? Will there come a time when I'll use this stuff and say, "Oh, this is why you've spent six, seven years staying up and writing these lessons out and driving back and forth to Berkeley three times a week?" ' But my insides would tell me, 'This is what you should be doing.' And now I can say, 'Yes! *This* is why I was doing it.' "

"What's the payoff?"

Long pause. . . "The fact that you're here. How's that? See, not only am I not just a drummer, I'm not just a musician either. I'm a person. A lot of things that are valid for me aren't only in musical terms. The fact that you're here and we're talking about what I've written, it tells me all those lessons have paid off, are bringing me attention, it shows me I've done things people are interested in."

"Well, I like the songs. They stay in my mind."

"I'm *glad*. And that's why I wanted to study. I wanted

to be able to write songs the way I knew I could, to present music my friends would like to hear, that would make people feel different things.

"So making the decision to study was easy. I make that kind of decision a lot. Moving to California was another of those things my insides told me to do. And after I got to California I decided to take swimming lessons. ["He did? Tony learned to swim? Aw, that's beautiful!"—Hancock.] I wanted to be able to go to a swimming pool and not just stand and wade; I got tired of going by the deep end and being scared. Now I can dive into the deep end. When I was in New York I was in therapy. In California, I have a therapist. It's helped me look at parts of my life I need to look at. It's the same kind of process—I'm always challenging myself to get better."

"Tony's composition, 'Sister Cheryl,'" says Herbie Hancock—"the first time I heard that tune [in 1982, when he and Williams played it on Wynton Marsalis's debut] I was shocked. Suddenly there was no more guesswork; Tony could really write chord changes. But what amazed me was that it was in a style that had eluded him for a long time. You know what Tony once told me? That he wanted to be able to write a tune anybody could sing, like a very natural kind of pop melody. Not that 'Sister Cheryl' is pop— it isn't—but it's catchy. Tony was always asking me what I thought of this or that tune that he wrote. See, I can write melodies people can sing. Tony could never do that, not till then. In many ways—though it's not all the same, and it's definitely Tony's writing—'Sister Cheryl' reminded me of 'Maiden Voyage.' It's one of my favorite compositions ever.

"The way he wrote it, you just move the bass line and the chord will change radically. It starts on a B-major chord, but using the second instead of the third. It's B, C-sharp, F-sharp. With so few notes in the chord, you get lots of flexibility. From B-major it goes to A-flat minor 7—and everything from that first chord fits with the second chord. Then you go to A with a B-major. That's the theme. Now, all these chords fit with the B, C-sharp and F-sharp of the first chord, so by changing the bass line you've changed all the chords, but kept the harmony hanging over from that very first chord. The melody moves, the bass moves, but the harmony stays the same; the outer part changes, the inner part doesn't. It's a nice piece of work."

"Tony's harmonies are like a breath of fresh air," says the Williams Quintet's fine pianist, Mulgrew Miller. "Remember, we're talking about a jazz composer who isn't himself a harmonic and melodic improviser. So his progressions may be a little unorthodox—Tony didn't learn jazz writing by playing 'Stardust.' The standard iii-vi-ii-V-I turnaround, there's none of that. You won't hear many 32-bar choruses either: as long as the song needs to be, that's how long he writes 'em. And the keys he chooses are somewhat unusual. 'Sister Cheryl,' that's in B-major. Outside of practicing scales, I'd never even played in B-major; it's mostly sharps. A piano player might fool around with something in B and say, 'Hmmm, I like this progression, I think I'll move it down to E-flat.' Not Tony—it's B.

"He's got a tremendous set of ears and he loves harmony; he loves the color of complex chords. Catchy melodies *are* one of his traits, but catchy melodies with complex harmonies. The chord progressions and chorus lengths are almost always unconventional. And that goes back to Wayne Shorter. Listen to Wayne's 'Nefertiti.' Most of his pieces with Miles were like that: simple melody, complex harmony. A piece of Tony's like 'Two Worlds' is so melodic, if someone heard only the melody, they'd have no idea what harmonic convulsions, what explosions, are going on underneath. Of all Tony's pieces, that's probably the meanest ["Every time I call 'Two Worlds,' " says Williams, "I see at least one guy scrambling for the sheet music"]: a lot of changes at a fast tempo, and they're complex changes, like G 9 to A-flat major 7 to B-flat 11 to B-minor flat 6th. The challenge to the improvisor is finding the continuity in all these changes that don't relate!

"I just think Tony hears something different from most people. He's got influences, like Wayne and Herbie and contemporary classical music, but mainly it just comes from being an inventive person. It's the same thing that lets him play the way he does. From what I hear, Tony was challenging the accepted forms right from his earliest days. Listen to those records with Eric Dolphy. It's clear that even at the age of eighteen he was an advanced thinker."

Tony Williams lit his third fat cigar in two hours. "It's a mark of a good song when anyone can play it, when it's so well-placed on the paper that it doesn't need a special interpretation, a great artist, to make it sound good." Brushing back the hotel-room curtain, he stood surveying Central Park West. He was beautifully dressed in a loose shirt, baggy winter pants and gorgeous two-toned shoes; circling his comfortable middle was the same metal-studded belt he'd worn the day before for his maiden voyage on David Letterman's TV show.

"It's like when you hear a hit song being played by some guy in a Holiday Inn bar and you say, 'Yeah, that's a great song.' Last night Paul Shaffer played 'Sister Cheryl' and it was a real turn-on. The song sounded so good. Those are good players, but what I'm saying is, the song translates easily from one group, one medium, to another; it doesn't take my band to play it.

"Or there's 'Native Heart'—the fact that I wrote that song [the title track on Williams's newest album] just knocks me out. It's like someone else wrote it and I'm getting a chance to play it. I worked on that song four, five months, playing it every day on the piano. It was *crafted*, like fine leather, like shoes."

"Could you analyze it for me?"

"No, I don't think I'd like to do that. Anyway, I can't. I write the songs and then I forget about them. It's up to the other guys to learn them. I don't need to. I'm playing the drums. Unless I'm working on a song, I can't tell you its chords; I'd have to go back to the piano with the music and I'd be able to play it after an hour or so. Besides, when you're writing, you have certain little things inside that tickle you, and you don't want to give them away. They wouldn't feel special if you flaunt them; it's like saying, 'Oooh, look how clever I am!' These things are private, they're little gems to me."

"But they're what's interesting: the things underneath."

"Yeah, and I'm interested in keeping them underneath. All I did in 'Native Heart' was invert the idea."

"Of the melody—?"

"Sort of."

"—or the chords?"

"Right."

"Which?"

[Coyly] "I don't want to give away all my secrets here! They're precious things!" Finally he relents. "Okay, what happened was, I had this idea and I wanted to make a song out of it." He sings a simple little eight-bar version of the melody. "In itself it was just an idea, just a real short thing. So first of all I had to weave length into it." Setting out, he broke the phrase into two-bar chunks and put a one-bar rest between each. More important, he rewrote it, introducing a subdominant in the eleventh measure so the tune didn't resolve so quickly. "All I did was put in a few new notes. And then the second time the phrase comes around, you go right to the five chord, the dominant—bang!—and it resolves. So I aired it out, fleshed it out, by putting in the subdominant.

"Okay, now I had to figure out, 'Where is this song going?' I had this two-note thing happening in the melody [D to A, a fifth]. Now, I deeply wanted the song to sound organic. So what I did was, I took that two-note phrase and gradually stretched it [to a sixth, F to D and then G to E] while slowing it down. Then I compressed it [accelerating it as it descends toward the tonic]—and when you compress a figure it brings a sense of resolution. So that was the work I did [in bars 25–33] to give the song a middle part, a so-called bridge, that sounded like it belonged, that was part of the opening melody." Just to strengthen the connection, Tony took a phrase from the fourth and fifth bars of the opening melody, turned the notes—B, C, D and B—upside down, and made this the last two bars of the middle: "a mirror, a reflective callback," as he puts it, of the opening melody.

All he needed now was an ending. "I was going to end it one way, with a little phrase that kind of drifts off. I decided that was too protracted, even though I liked the phrase." So he wrote another ending: the opening melody, but with a few new intervals and one brand-new note, an A-flat: "It's a piece of music, and a note, that's never been heard in the song before, so it really puts a cap on things. And then I said, 'Hey, wait a minute'—and I took that first ending, the one I'd loved but hadn't used, and made it the intro and outro. It was perfect there." And he had his song: a sultry, moodily swirling 45-measure composition, patiently teased from an eight-bar scrap.

"I think more about these kinds of things than I do about drums. 'Cause like I said, the drumming has never been a problem for me. That was the problem! I felt like all everybody wanted was this drummer, that Tony Williams was not there, that I didn't matter. And it caused me a lot of emotional pain.

"I'm not talking about fans, I'm talking about people I worked with. That was the pain, that if I weren't this drummer I wouldn't have these people as my friends. And I realized that was true. Everything that went on told me that. There I was in New York by myself—seventeen, eighteen, nineteen—and the only reason I was here was because I played the drums as well as I did. It was strange, very strange. In Miles Davis's band I was the youngest, the smallest and, as I felt, the least educated. I didn't feel good about myself. So that's to answer your question why would a person who's good at one thing want to be good at something else too. And those are valid reasons.

"I'd like to write things I wouldn't have to play. I'd like to write for certain orchestras. I've never been the type that needed to play drums in order to feel like a person. I *choose* to play, it's my *desire* to play. I'm not the kind of guy that goes around with drumsticks in his hands beating on things. I could live without drumming. There was a couple of years when I didn't play at all; I just hung out, lived off the rent from a house I own uptown here. Because I don't need the drums, I think I play better. I respect them too much to use them as a crutch. When I sit down at the drums it's because I want to; it's like 'I'm here to be your friend.'

"The drums *are* my best friend. The drums are the only thing I've been able to count on totally, except my mother—and sometimes when she gets pissed off, boy, she can give me a *look*. . . . If it weren't for the drums, I wouldn't be here. But I can listen to the drums in my head. I mean, I rarely, in the last ten years, get the feeling to just go downstairs and play drums. I never practice. I can not play for a year and it'll only take me a night or two to get back to where I was. After thirty-six years, there's a certain level you won't never go below."

Which leaves him free to chase his new passion. Last autumn, in "one of the most thrilling experiences I've ever had," Williams performed his first extended composition, the fifteen-minute "Rituals: Music for Piano, String Quartet, Drums and Cymbals," with the Kronos Quartet and Hancock. He's sniffing out the world of soundtracks: "I'd do basically anything, movies, TV, jingles, just to see how it came out." The quintet, finally getting its due as one of the best of jazz's small groups, is always digesting some new Williams piece, and he's also writing for an electric band (sax, guitar, keyboards, bass, and drums) he plans to start.

"The more I write, the easier it comes. And it's really a pleasure to be able to write something, have it make sense, and then *play* it: to have it be not just an exercise but something the other guys enjoy playing. That's more important to me than just being able to say 'I wrote this.'

"I'm really surprised I've had the emotional stamina to stay resilient. Especially considering how burnt out I was feeling maybe fifteen years ago. It took courage to put a band together when no one else was doing it, and to write all the music. I've had to put myself out there for the scrutiny of everyone, to write songs everyone would scrutinize and criticize and review and critique. That's something that's very scary. To have done it, and to have gotten the reaction I've had, has been very, very wonderful."

"But it shouldn't have been scary, you'd been writing for years."

"What do you mean 'shouldn't have been'? It just was. Like I said, my writing was not the kind of writing I would have wanted it to be. Now it is. But I had to trust that. So now, I've finally gained trust in these other parts of myself.

I'm not just 'Tony Williams, drummer.' And that feels pretty neat."

WILLIAMS TELLS

Tony writes on a Baldwin grand piano or on an airplane. He plays the same fire-engine yellow Gretsch drums he's used for years; in fact, Gretsch calls the color "Tony Williams Yellow Lacquer." He owns a half-dozen identical kits, including one he keeps in Europe. The snare is 6½" deep, the rack tom-toms are 9" × 13" and 10" × 14", the three floor toms are 14" × 14", 16" × 16" and 16" × 18" and the bass drum is 14" × 24". Tony's Zildjian cymbals — all K's except for the hi-hat — are 18" and 20" crashes, a 16" light ride and a 22" medium ride. The hi-hat cymbals are 15" heavies. Though he hasn't used a drum machine since borrowing a Linn for "Geo Rose" on 1987's *Civilization*, he owns a bunch: an E-mu SP1200 sampling drum machine, Simmons SDS 5 and SDS 7 electronic drums, a Simmons MTM MIDI trigger, and "an old Oberheim [a DMX] and an old Roland drum machine." Add an E-Max digital sampling rack, E-mu Emulator II sampling keyboard, Macintosh SE and Mac Plus computers, a Sony TV and a 1990 535i BMW, and you've got the very model of a well-heeled hedonistic turn-of-the-century jazz artiste.

—May 1991

DIZZY GILLESPIE:

THE LION IN WINTER

BY CHIP
STERN

With rolling lawns, majestic driveways and obligatory collections of pricey cars, a series of splendid homes adorns Palisades Avenue, the main drag heading out towards Englewood, New Jersey. Here, where the reet meet the elite, resides one John Birks Gillespie: musical innovator, spiritual catalyst, twentieth-century revolutionary, still the road warrior and globe-trotting ambassador of America's classical music. Crossing the railroad tracks into downtown, the city appears a healthy tintype of Main Street U.S.A., its center dominated by a thirties public works-style municipal building. The scene brings to mind the considerably humbler environs of Cheraw, South Carolina, where Gillespie grew up, and the many roads since traveled that have brought him to this place.

Leaning against a street sign, I'm comforted to think that at least one of the good guys got a taste, got his due, and that, closing in on seventy-five, he's still going strong. Recent evidence includes such fine albums as *Max + Dizzy: Paris 1989*, an improvised encounter with the percussion master, and *Live at the Royal Festival Hall*, a big band/percussion date that reinforces his stature as composer and soloist. Not to mention his touring. For Dizzy Gillespie never stops working. Never. "I don't even look at my itinerary," he'd said over the phone. "Ask me where am I goin' and when I'm goin'? I don't know. The most I've been off now that I can recall was four weeks early in January [1991] when I had my cataracts operated on. Other than that, I always go. I take what I want and leave with it."

He'd just completed a week's engagement, sold out, at New York's prestigious Blue Note with his superb working band (featuring tenor discovery Ronald Holloway, who calls forth visions of Johnny Griffin and Sonny Rollins, and seasoned campaigners Ignacio Berroa, John Lee and Ed Cherry). He's planning a return in January '92 for a month of special appearances, with a different grouping each week, including an all-star ensemble, Latin band and his United Nations Big Band. In between, the road beckons.

Waiting on Birks to show, my eyes alight on a yellow-painted curb across from City Hall, signifying no parking. The sign above bears a more pointed message: DIZZY'S PLACE. Now, that's respect. Suddenly someone arrives from behind and snaps at my suspenders. "I'd have come into Manhattan to pick you up, man, but my wife won't let me take her car across the bridge," he says, sounding like a kid caught with his hand in the cookie jar. A grin lights up that enormous face, suggesting Jabba the Hutt. It is the face of a man who never forgot what it felt like to be a child—perhaps not unlike his baby brother Miles. Yet where that reflective Mr. Davis seemed to ruminate on the hurts, the exuberant Mr. Gillespie reminisces on the joy. For a few seconds all I can do is stare—this is a boyhood hero—and soon find myself doing a Ralph Kramden routine, *a-hum-na-hum-na-hum-na*, tongue-tied in his presence.

"You know, Diz, this'll sound funny, but I'm a little intimidated by you, man."

"Hahaha, get outta here," Dizzy chortles, with a good-natured slap on the back for punctuation. "I'm no old what do you call 'em, those guys that sit out in the deserts ... old masters. I'm still a learner, just like you."

His car—his wife Lorraine's car—is a Mercedes 250 CES, a classic set of wheels. "I bought this new back in 1966, same time we bought our house. Before that we lived in Corona, Queens, for years, a block away from Louis Armstrong." He reaches to the floor and picks up what appears to be a carved walking stick, embellished in a vaguely Mediterranean design. "Open it up," he suggests, and it turns out to be a kind of scabbard, revealing a short, nasty-looking blade.

"The equalizer, huh, Diz?"

"Yeaaaaahhh," he drawls. "Sometimes you'll be driving around here, and people are crazy, man, they'll just cut you off and think nothin' of it. One day these guys cut me off and I beep as they go by. When we come to the light, he starts to get out of his car, so I showed him this, you believe it, and that was that."

"Sort of like when Cab Calloway called you out in front of the band," I respond, referring to an incident in the

1930s where the heigh-de-ho man confronted a young Gillespie for allegedly throwing spitballs during his performance. And got his ass cut in the bargain. Gillespie giggles at the memory. "Cut his ass. Shit, I was tryin' to *kill* his ass. My blade was open before it left my pocket. We're tight now, though," he adds as an afterthought. "He realizes that he was wrong; he was accusin' me of somethin' I didn't do."

Diz turns off Palisades Avenue, proceeding through some wooded areas and along a meandering series of comfortable-looking streets and homes. "See this?" He beams, pointing to a street sign. "Here's Hollywood, and here's Vine. Somebody asks where you live, you tell 'em Hollywood and Vine."

All right, say something. "Sure is nice here. Do you ever get to enjoy this? Are you afraid if you come off of the road you'll lose your lip or something?"

"No, I'm not afraid. I play every day anyway. Always playin' out and gettin' paid for it, at least two hundred days a year. That's why I haven't written anything in a *long* time. One time I was worried about my jaws, because when I do this"—Dizzy presses forefinger to embouchure, expanding those famous cheeks to roughly the size of a bowling ball— "there's a strain, and I thought my cheeks might give out. But when I do that—push it in, go on, put your strongest finger here and try and push in." His cheek resists my finger with the tensile strength of a bear's belly. "So, I don't think they're goin' to give out for a long time, as hard as they get."

"Did you always play the horn like that?"

"No, no. I started doing it about thirty years later. Not having had a teacher was the trouble; you try anything. Lorraine say, 'Hmmm, looks like your cheeks are coming out.' Before I knew it they were out like this.

"You know, the trumpet de-*mands* your time. Practice:

252

That does it. You need to know exactly where you put your mouthpiece—got to be the same place all the time. That's what I work on. It always kicks your ass. You get a little better, but not too much.

"I have a regimen to warm up, yes. Whole tones. Starting at low G, you go up to C, and you come back down to G. Sometime you do scales in thirds or fourths going up and coming down, sometimes fast, sometimes real slow. The idea is to get the sound of the notes properly. See, I asked a classical musician once, a very famous cat. I said, 'Do you practice?' He said, 'Every day.' I said, 'What if you didn't?' He said, 'Well, after one day you will notice you should have practiced; two days, your compatriots will notice; three days, the whole world will notice.' I don't practice exactly the way I did when I was coming up, but pretty close."

"So you've learned to pace yourself on the horn," I propose, "sort of like Sugar Ray or Muhammad Ali when they got older and didn't have those young legs to carry them. Rope-a-dope, right?"

Dizzy laughs. "You don't look at an instrument as a physical thing of fighting somebody. It's about finesse with this"—he points to his brain. "You got to work out your ideas. Then there's no telling how long you can play, with the proper feelings.

"Sometimes you surprise yourself, let me tell you," he enthuses, gripping the steering wheel a little tighter. "This past spring I played on that boat ride around Manhattan with my band, like I'd never played before! I'd gone to the dentist and had this tooth worked on; it was loose, and he tightened it up. On that boat ride, everything I *thought* I wanted to play came out." He shakes his head, amazed. "I haven't played like that, boy . . . I never remember playing like that."

He pulls into the driveway of a long, capacious ranch-style house and eases into the garage, pointing out a white mark on the wall that lets him know when he's in danger of totalling the front end. Along the wall are trap cases bearing his name, packed and waiting—whatcha doing home, man? Entering the kitchen from the garage, I can hear Lorraine's voice in the distance, dishing the dirt about the Clarence Thomas hearings with a friend on the phone. Their living room is laid out to emphasize its spaciousness—the kind of simple understatement only money can buy—and no one needs to say that it is set aside for special occasions. I pull a dozen roses out of my bag for Diz to give Lorraine, as he motions down to the basement.

If the rest of the house is Lorraine's domain, the expansive basement—with its wood panels, small bar, pool table, upright piano, television, synthesizer, drum machine, eight-track recorder and ancient stereo—is clearly Diz's crib, part rehearsal space, part rec room. In one corner is a 28-inch Wuhan Chinese cymbal, a real beast, and a set of golden-chrome Remo drums, compliments of Louie Bellson. There's a JVC compact stereo—still in its box—that someone has sent to Diz, he can't recall who. "People are always sending me stuff," he says simply, and offers his guest a drink.

"I was born October twenty-first, 1917. I always thought I was a musician. Thought I was a musician before I really *was* a musician. At first I had a trombone—*I* had no trombone, but I had the school's horn, you see. That was the only thing left. I played on it the best I could. I was *little*. I was only eleven-and-a-half, and my arms weren't long enough to make that stretch, so I could only reach a few of them positions. Didn't have a trumpet. Boy next door, Brother Hampton, he let me practice on his trumpet. So, by the time I put the trombone down, I could play a little bit in B flat.

"What happened next, a guy named Sonny Matthews came back home. Sonny was an experienced musician who took lessons from his mother and he played some piano, too. Well, he knew who I was, because everybody knows one another in Cheraw. And then his grandmother was Miss Bates. We went to the same church, and every Sunday morning I'd be there waitin' to help Miss Bates out with her cane. I was very close to that family.

"So this big guy came and got me: 'Hey, Sonny Matthews wants to see you.' 'Ahhh, yeah,' I said, 'okay.' I'm a little cocky—and here I know only one key. Sonny sat at the piano and said, 'Well, whatta ya wanna play?' I said, 'What d'you know?' He called 'Nagasaki'—but I only know the B flat key, and he calls it in C. Man, I couldn't find one note. He said, 'Something must be wrong.' I was cryin' an' everything, and I thought, 'How'm I ever gonna pick myself up and be a musician?'

"So I learned how to read. My father had a whole band in the house, almost. He had a piano, a bass violin—only had one string, but then we only played in B flat anyway. I taught myself all the chords and voicings and inversions on that piano, by myself. No teachers. We didn't have no books. All the schools were segregated. I learned how to read and started playin' at home. Later, I taught all the piano players how to play the comp—the accompaniment—in our music. But I never tried to really play the piano, I wanted to play the trumpet. I'd heard Roy Eldridge on the radio—on somebody *else's* radio. I was playing a little bit by that time, and I didn't know Louis Armstrong. Roy Eldridge, he was my man—I tried to copy his whole thing.

"The trombone player where I went to school in Cheraw, Bill MacNeil, reminded me of J. C. Higginbotham, real rough, you know, growling cat. He got caught peekin' in the white homes around there." There's a short pause, and Dizzy's voice trails off, grows distant. "They killed him. Bill MacNeil . . . Bill MacNeil . . . he must have been about eighteen years old then or something, you know."

It's a poignant moment. Gillespie's music has always been a freedom song, pointing to an imagined future of incredible beauty, transcending the ignorance of cracker conventions, even as it signaled black people to get out of the way, too, something new is coming through. Transforming the bluesiness and locomotion of swing-era dances into a deep, dignified modern concert music, it's full of joys and dangers. In Dizzy's hands it's been less a stage for protest than for affirmation. But if he's too proud to wear the scars of Dixie on his sleeve, the memories linger, whispering of how far we've come, how far we have to go.

"I was back in Cheraw for a Dizzy Gillespie Day, and the mayor invited me to a cocktail party in his house," he recalls. "So I thought I'd get a haircut. I went into a barber shop in town, and the guy told me, 'We don't cut colored hair.' Ain't that a bitch? And I'm definitely the most well-known person ever to come out of Cheraw. I told the mayor that, and he was shocked: 'He can't do that.' Mmmmm.

"Racism? I grew up with it. I remember it stopped me from playin' with a little boy named John Burrell; he was my little pal then, and his mother and father said, 'Now, look, you can't play with that boy no more.' Then there was a white boy, Kenny McManus. His family had two swimmin' pools: a white one and a black one. It's where I used to swim and dive when I was little, might have been ten, eleven. I used to dive for money, off a high buildin' up there, coulda broke my neck. But I was a daredevil. I've been a daredevil all my life, really. They'd say I was 'bad,' you know, but they called me by my name. I'd always get into trouble, fightin' every day in school.

"Damn, when I think how close I came to being hitched up behind a plow, man. I finally got out of Cheraw when my mother moved to Philadelphia my last year in school, and soon as summertime came, I hitched a ride up. And I stayed till I moved to New York in '37. The first week there, got a job for eight dollars a week. Yeah, big money. I don't know how many clothes I bought off that, all Parisian tailored stuff, on time. I'd pay a dollar-and-a-half a week."

That era also provided Gillespie with the best possible training grounds for a young player—the big bands. Within those juggernauts he learned the craft of his horn, how to play lead and in a section, and was tested every night by his fellow trumpet players in countless styles. A few years later Teddy Hill, in whose band Diz first traveled to Paris, began booking a Harlem club called Minton's, which became the crucible for a fiery new musical language known as bebop. Dizzy, of course, was present at the creation.

"Oh, that was some time, boy. We'd go in there and then we'd go to the Uptown House after that, and you'd come out in the daylight. That band was Nick Fenton on bass, Kenny Clarke on drums, Monk was on piano, Joe Guy on trumpet and Kermit Scott on sax. Charlie Christian used to come all the time. He left his amplifier down there when he died. Old guys didn't come down too much, except Roy, he could make it. Me, Charlie Shavers and 'Bama—Carl Wooley—all three of us would jump on Roy, gang up on him," he laughs at the memory. "Of course, Roy'd come through the door hitting high C after high C from the first note, an' he was ready to take on *all* comers. He was the most competitive man you ever met, oooohweeeee!

"Monk was the most individual player who came through. Monk with the minor-sixth with the sixth in the bass: He taught us that chord. We used to change stuff to keep guys who couldn't play off the bandstand. In the daytime I'd call Monk and say, 'Hey, listen to this.' I learned 'How High the Moon' from Nat Cole, who was playin' at Kelly's Stables. 'What's the name of that number, Nat? Play that for me again. Damn, them keys are movin'.' And I hurried to Minton's, showed that to Monk. We would make numbers up, but with standards, we'd change them around, put in new melodies and have a new tune. Like 'Groovin' High' came out of 'Whispering.'

"Somewhere in there I met Charlie Parker. He was with Jay McShann, I was with Cab. This was what, 1939, '40? Buddy Anderson took me to see him. We played at the Booker Washington Hotel. When I first heard Charlie Parker play, *his* style was basically there. He played *tunes inside of tunes*. And the chords were the correct ones, too. Man, he was cute, all right.

"Now you see, my training was a little more sophisticated than Charlie Parker's, harmonically. I showed him a lotta things on the piano. But Charlie Parker had the style of gettin' those notes *out*! And the way that he got from one note to another, the way that he set 'em up—nobody'd ever done nothin' like that before.

"We were all tryin' to play like Charlie Parker. That's why you can't tell who's who on some of them early records, like that Metronome All-Star date with me'n Miles and Fats Navarro. Even I can't tell who's playing what. All the trumpet players of that time tried to play like him. But Charlie Parker was indescribable. . . . 'You took advantage of my friend, you cur,' " he chuckles, recalling an incident where Bird confronted a redneck who'd gone upside Dizzy's head with a bottle. "Mmm, mmm . . . a spiritual man."

Though Diz and Bird were the priest and prophet of bebop, they went separate ways off the bandstand, and their differing lifestyles pulled them apart at times. "Because Charlie Parker used dope—they said—all the young musicians who wanted to follow Charlie Parker went that way: like Miles, Sonny Rollins, Sonny Stitt, J. J. Johnson, Fats Navarro. They all felt that would help them—hah hah hah. I mean, we were brothers. But he was the one who was interested in that. He never offered me none. And I never saw him do it."

Diz wanders off upstairs to check in with Lorraine, the

anchor who helps him stay focused, who kept his other life together while Gillespie led his great big bands of the forties and fifties and expanded on the Afro-Cuban and Latin innovations he introduced to modern jazz through his association with Mario Bauza and Chano Pozo. When he returns downstairs with a big case, I've started to unpack and set up his new stereo. The technology fascinates him, particularly the compact discs.

"How many of those you get in that little drawer, there?"

"One at a time seems to work best, Diz." He unpacks his case to appraise a new gold-plated trumpet from Martin, engraved with his name and otherwise busy with ornate detail. The Dizzy bell points up at a 45-degree angle. "Don't play no regular horn anymore," he explains. "The sound is prettier to my ear when it's less direct."

He takes out the mouthpiece and begins warming his lip with bends and shakes and long tones that sound like soulful duck calls. Now and then he pauses to pick up and admire the new horn, check out the action; then he returns to the mouthpiece. Finally he puts them together and runs through pedal tones and scales with the mute, finishing with several of his melodies on the open horn.

"Yeaaaah," he says, fingering the valves, "when she gets broken in, a few weeks down the road, this is going to be a nice horn."

"Sounds like she blows real easy, Diz."

He fixes me with a stagey stare. "Sheeeeeet. Ain't none of them blow easy," he laughs, and starts in again with more purpose. At times he stops and yawns, then jumps back in; got to stay on that horn. Maybe I'm beginning to wear too, with this "tell me all about 1941" line, and here we are in 1991. I pack up so that he can get on and rest.

It's dark as he backs out of the driveway. "Maybe next time I'll get to say hello to Lorraine," I suggest.

"Sure, man," Diz nods. "She really appreciated them flowers. What people don't understand about Lorraine, her being so strong and all, is that she's really very shy. I've always felt comfortable around people, but sometimes I'm too trusting. But Lorraine, man, no one can put anything over on her."

"Does she follow the Baha'i faith also?"

"Noooo," he says gravely. "She's a devoted Roman Catholic. She thinks Baha'i is some kind of weird religion out the jungle. I just say to her, 'Now you take care of yours and I will take care of mine—' "

"—and I'll meet you at the finish line?"

"Yeah. She believes all of this about Jesus, how he brought somebody up from the dead, and he died and went to heaven and come back. I don't see no sense in making all that happen to make you live a full life. I don't exactly believe in heaven and hell. But I believe that there is a Being somewhere that can create miracles over here and in the outer realms. I'm a believer. I believe in God.

"I was raised Methodist, but I never followed any one religion. I read some of the Koran, like I read the Bible and other books. The Baha'i religion came out of Islam—all religions are similar, but these two are closer together. It originates with this very religious Muslim in Persia during the last part of the past century. He started preaching that now is the time for a new message from God. Well, you know how the Muslims felt about that, because they think God's not going to talk to mankind no more after the Koran. They think that's the last message we're going to get. But I don't know why God would stop now. If God was that intelligent, how could he give you everything he'd want you to know in that little time?"

How indeed? But then, among God's more sublime miracles, John Birks Gillespie must rank up there with sunsets and tax refunds. For Dizzy is all about music and spirit.

Simple as that, and if Charlie Parker came down with the word, Dizzy made it into flesh, gave it substance and, for fifty years on, has been performing and teaching it to succeeding generations of jazz musicians. His innovations remain the cornerstone of almost everything we play.

Dimly through these reflections, it occurs to me that we've been circling these streets for several minutes. "Yeah," Diz confirms absentmindedly, "I don't do much driving at night. Can't hardly read them street signs."

He tries another route but ends up in the same place. Diz makes a U-turn and doubles back around, cruising past an enormous California-style house, enclosed by high stucco walls.

"You know who's supposed to have bought that house and be movin' in? The Boss."

"Bruce . . . ?"

"Yeaaahhhh. You think that's something, Eddie Murphy's got him like a seven-million dollar estate up around here that's something else. Oooooweeee!"

Dizzy stops to inspect a street sign and regain his bearings. He clucks his tongue and shakes his head as he makes another attempt to reach Palisades Avenue. At the next corner there's a middle-aged couple out on the street, unpacking their car from a shopping trip. Diz rolls down his window. "Excuse me," he says, beckoning, and there's a giddy glint of recognition in their eyes.

"Answer me this. How can you be driving around only a block from where you live and be so totally lost?"

They double over with laughter. They're still laughing as we drive off.

—*March 1992*